What They Didn't Teach You in **Spanish** Class

What They Didn't Teach You in **Spanish** Class

Slang phrases for the café, club, bar, bedroom, game and more

Juan Caballero

ULYSSES PRESS

Published by:
Ulysses Press
PO Box 3440
Berkeley, CA 94703
www.ulyssespress.com

ISBN: 978-1-64604-395-8 (paperback)
ISBN: 978-1-61243-675-3 (hardback)
Library of Congress Control Number: 2016957691

Printed in the United States
10 9 8 7 6 5 4 3 2 1

Managing editor: Claire Chun
Editors: Shayna Keyles, Alice Riegert
Proofreader: Lauren Harrison
Design and illustrations: what!design @ whatweb.com
Production: Yesenia Garcia-Lopez

IMPORTANT NOTE TO READERS: This book is independently authored and published. No endorsement or sponsorship by or affiliation with movies, celebrities, products, or other copyright and trademark holders is claimed or suggested. All references in this book to copyrighted or trademarked characters and other elements of movies and products are for the purpose of commentary, criticism, analysis, and literary discussion only.

To my father, who taught me the lurid joys of profanity;
to my mother, who taught me the inward satisfaction of pedagogy;
and to you, dear reader, for paying me to combine the two.

Contents

Using This Book

This book was written with the assumption that you already took a fair number of adequate Spanish classes, and already know how to speak the language itself, at least in its abstract, off-the-rack form. This is a book designed to take your Spanish to the next level, out into the real world, and cannot be as precise or definitive as a language textbook because it is a pile of examples to help you figure out always-contextual and ever-changing slang. So if you're looking for a grammar lesson or a universal phrase book, you're in the wrong spot. But if you want to tell your friend that he has a tiny dick or to get rid of the douchebag hitting on you in the bar, this is the book for you.

Every phrase in this book is in current usage, and most of it isn't in dictionaries even though it's widely used and understood. Except in special cases, the English is given first, followed by the Spanish. Sometimes the Spanish is given with alternatives (*gordo/a, tu/s*) to account for gender or plural differences. This isn't a grammar book and you're not an idiot, so we expect that you'll be able to figure it out without any more explanation.

Unlike other volumes in the *What They Didn't Teach You in Class* series, this book covers not one language, but many. That's because Spanish is not universal. The slang and casual language you'll hear in Colombia is quite different from what you might hear in Spain or Mexico. Most of what's included here was chosen because it's easily understood in any Spanish-speaking country, but there are many terms that are region- or country-specific. For all of those, we've indicated, in parentheses, in which region or country the phrase is most commonly used:

COUNTRY	ABBREVIATION
Latin America	LatAm
South America	S.Am
Central America	CenAm
Southern Cone	S.Cone (Argentina, Chile, and Uruguay)
Caribbean	Carib
Andes	Andes
Mexico	Mex
Guatemala	Gua
El Salvador	ElS
Honduras	Hon
Nicaragua	Nic
Costa Rica	CoR
Panama	Pan
Cuba	Cub
Dominican Republic	DoR
Puerto Rico	PuR
Venezuela	Ven
Colombia	Col
Ecuador	Ecu
Peru	Per
Bolivia	Bol
Chile	Chi
Paraguay	Par
Uruguay	Uru
Argentina	Arg
Spain	Spn

Whenever a regional term is given in addition to a universal one, you can assume it'll sound natural to someone from that region to hear that term. However, many regional words are rapidly becoming international, as Latin American media culture continues to globalize, and as teenagers everywhere stream music and TV shows from around the Spanish-speaking globe.

If personal curiosity or professional demands require you to know exactly where a given term is used, or if you want to dive deeper into the seedy world of Spanish slang, the easiest place to start is online. Here are some resources:

www.rae.es—The Real Academia Española's online dictionary may not always be cutting-edge for Latin American slang, but at least it's reliable and accurate.

www.jergasdehablahispana.org—Roxana Fitch's invaluable, free, and searchable dictionary houses a massive collection of slang, sorted by region.

forum.wordreference.com—The Word Reference forums are a thriving international community of professional translators and amateur linguists, where you can get answers from real people in the field.

The best language teacher, however, will always be immersion. So get to traveling, do some downloading, start YouTube-ing, or, at the very least, go to the Hispanic part of town and strike up some conversations—just don't start with what you learned in the Smack Talk chapter!

Now plow through this quickly as a starting point and get out there and get creative—real Spanish isn't in a book, it's on the lips of the drunk people, scrawled on bathroom walls, and muttered in your ear by the guy next to you in the back of cop car.

Pronouncing Spanish

Speaking Spanish like a *pinche gringo* will make you seem like, well, a *pinche gringo*, and will raise the price of everything you want to buy in proportion to how annoying your accent is. It can even mark you as an easy target for pickpockets or muggers. So get your pronunciation straight. You have three golden rules to remember:

1. Watch your damn vowels already! Each vowel is essentially the same in every context:

A is always like the "a" in "father."

O is always like the "o" in "bone."

I is always like the "ie" in "wiener."

E is always like the "e" in "wet."

U is always like the "oo" in "poon," unless it comes after a "g" or a "q" and has no umlaut dots over it, in which case it's silent.

One of the biggest slipups that English speakers make when speaking Spanish is following the unconscious English pronunciation rules that make vowels change contextually, smuggling in foreign A's and turning every unstressed vowel into the "uuuuh" sound that Spanish speakers equate with the pronunciation of a village idiot (don't pruhtend you don't know whuht I'm talking uhbout).

2. Most consonants are the same as English, but a few can really trip you up. G's are pronounced like an English G before A, U, Ü, or O, but before E and I, they sound more like an English H (so does an X, by the way). J's are like English H's but pushed further back in the throat, which you may notice people clearing their throats or some native speakers of Hebrew or Arabic doing in English. H's are always silent, and if you pronounce them, it's a dead giveaway that you're just starting out, and will often get you "Oh, honey" looks. D's and R's before vowels are hard to pronounce quickly and lightly enough. K's, hard C's, T's, and P's aren't aspirated as they are in English (aspiration is that puff of air you feel if you hold your hand in front of your mouth and pronounce "pop" and

"totally" in any North American accent). If your teachers taught you to pronounce your Z's as TH's in Spanish and you're anywhere outside of Spain, stop that right away; it's not going to go well for you. Pay attention to local LL pronunciation, because it varies wildly not just by geography but also by context (between casual speech and singing, for instance). Similarly, how hard people roll their RRs (and whether they roll Rs at the beginning of words for clarity and emphasis) varies too much for general rules to be helpful.

3. Pay attention to accents when learning new words, and review the accent rules online or in your old grammar book before traveling. If you put the accent on the wrong syllable, people think you're saying another word, which, 99 percent of the time, will be a word that doesn't exist. Americans are often shocked by not being understood for having fudged such a "minor" detail. But it makes a major difference to Spanish speakers, so they, in turn, feel shocked when Americans walk around speaking gibberish and getting impatient with people.

4. Don't overpronounce. Pay attention to local pronunciation and try to keep up; it makes you sound natural and cool. Vowels and syllables sometimes drop out of the middle of long words (*no te pr'ocupes*). D's between vowels at the end of words often drop out to make a vowel diphthong (it's *complicao*). Consonants at the end of words in an unstressed syllable, particularly D's and S's, often get underpronounced or forgotten altogether (*de vera', no te procupa'*).

In the Caribbean, this process is taken one step further, frequently coming right in the middle of a word (*¡Tú huele' com'u' pe'cao!*). Also, syllable emphasis can change from city to city, overriding the normal accent-placement of a word. Similarly, subtle slipups like mixing up the pronunciation between S and Z or T and D, however the word might actually be spelled, can mark you as foreign. So listen closely to how people pronounce words you thought you already knew.

CHAPTER 1

Meet & Greet
Los Coloqueos

Spanish speakers in a friendly (or alcoholic) environment rarely start conversations with an *Hola* or *Buen día*. It's more casual and common to head straight for a question, even if it hangs in the air as hypothetical and unanswered; as in English, it's also not that strange to answer a question like *¿Qué onda?* with...*the same exact question.*

What's up?
¿Qué tal?

What'd I miss?
¿Qué pasó?; ¿Quihubo?

What's up guys?
¿Qué hay de nuevo, muchachos?

What up?
¿Qué onda?

What's goin' on?
¿Qué sapa?
Qué pasa in corny anagram.

What're you up to?
¿Qué haces?

WHAT'S UP?
¿QUÉ TAL?

¿Qué tal-co? (S.Cone)

¿Qué tal andas? (Spn)

¿Qué jais? (Mex)

¿Qué volá? (Carib)

¿Qué más? (Andes)

¿Qué's la que hay? (PuR)

What's the good word, Fatty?

¿Qué dices, Gordo?

Many greetings sound best followed by an affectionate, mildly offensive epithet (Tubby, Pizzaface, Nancy, Bigballs, whatever).

Whatcha got?

¿A ver?

What the cock (have you been up to)?

¿A verga?

What else is new with you?

De tu vida, ¿qué más?

How you doing?
¿Cómo andas?

Once you're done with the initial niceties and greetings, it's time to dig a little deeper and inquire about the person's life. Vague, fragmentary answers are the norm, so don't expect a lengthy response, or even a complete sentence.

How are you?

¿Cómo estás?

How's it goin'?

¿Cómo te va?; ¿Cómo le va?

To be chummy but still respectful, use the second one.

How you doin'?

¿Cómo andas? | *¿Cómo andamio?* (S.Cone)

How's life?
¿Cómo anda la vida?

How 'bout things with you?
¿Y tus cosas?

> **Kickin' ass!**
> *¡De pelos! | ¡A toda madre!* (Mex) | *¡De butaca!* (S.Cone)
>
> **Straight chillin'.**
> *¡Todo tránqui'!*
>
> **I'm all right.**
> *Ando ahí nomás.*
>
> **It's all good!**
> *Todo [va] bien.*
>
> **Same as ever.**
> *Como siempre.*
>
> **Still kicking around here, aren't I?**
> *Sigo por aquí, no?*
>
> **Still here.**
> *Aquí nomás.*
>
> **Everything's super.**
> *Todo a full. | ...full de to'.* (Carib)
>
> **Fine.**
> *En marcha.*
>
> **Never better.**
> *Nunca mejor.*
>
> **Great.**
> *A todo dar.* (LatAm)
>
> **Super.**
> *De órdago.* (Spn)
>
> **Awesome.**
> *Increíble. | Guay.* (Spn)

I can't complain.
No me quejo.

It is what it is.
Es lo que sea.

It's whatever.
Me da lo mismo.

Shitty.
Una cagada.

Fucking crappy.
Como el orto. (S.Am)

Fucked up.
Jodido.

I'm in a bad fucking mood.
Vengo encabronado.

Estoy encabronado would be more literal, but *vengo* is kind of a warning to the listener that the bad mood's been on for a while.

How's life, really?
¿Pero en serio, cómo te va la vida?

Even if your friend didn't mention any girl/boy/work/family troubles last time you talked, it's fair game to ask them about it point-blank if you've heard things through the grapevine.

What's the deal with…?
¿Qué onda con…?

What's the latest with…?
¿Qué cuentas sobre…?; ¿Qué se cuenta de…?

> **your old lady**
> *la vieja*

> **the ball-n-chain**
> *la jefa*

the ball-buster
la domadora
literally, "stud-breaker"

Captain Dudepants
el capitán

Main Fellow
el mariscal

your folks
los viejos | *los tatas* (Mex)

The whole situation is **seriously fucked**.
*Todo el asunto está **seriamente jodido**.*

I don't even wanna talk about it.
Ni hablar.

What's happenin' with that **little venture**?
*¿Que pasó con ese **bisnes**?*

How'd that **gig** work out?
*¿Qué pasó con ese **curro**?* (Spn) | *...esa **chamba**?* (Mex) |
*...esa **changa**?* (S.Cone) | *...ese **camello**?* (Andes)

Gettin' paid, at least.
Me pagan, por lo menos.

They're really **wiping their asses** with me.
*Me están **pasando por el culo**.*

Clueless
Despistado

I dunno...
No sé...

I don't know what to tell you.
No sabría qué decirte.

I have no clue.
No tengo ni idea.

I have no fucking idea.
Ni puta idea.

What do I know?
¿Qué se yo?

God only knows.
Sepa el Señor.

How **the fuck** would I know?
*¿Y yo, **qué mierda** sé?* | *...**qué coño***... (Spn, Carib) |
*...**qué cojones**...* (Mex)

Who knows?
*Sepa **Fulano**.* | *...Pancha.* (Mex) |*...Moya.* (Chi)
Literally, "Random dude knows."

Fucked if I know.
¡Sepa la bola! | *...la chingada!* (Mex)

....

Look who showed up!
¡Mira quién apareció!

It's common among good friends to express exaggerated surprise
or joy at an arrival, particularly a late one. These expressions seem
dramatic in English, but they are a normal part of interacting in
Spanish-speaking lands. It's common in these situations to call
someone by a nickname that would, in other contexts, be way
more offensive, like *pendejo de mierda* (total fucker) or *hijo de la
gran puta* (son of a royal whore).

Long time no see!
¡Tanto tiempo!

You made it, dummy!
*¡**Caíste**, salame!* (S.Cone)

They let you out!
¡Te dejaron salir!

DID I STUTTER?
¿TARTAMUDEO?

There's lots of meaningless filler-words that people use to "um" and "uh" their way to an answer, particularly to a question they find too direct. In informal settings, talk radio, and TV news, you hear these all the time, often unconsciously peppered throughout everything people say.

...I guess...
...o sea...

...I mean...
...digo...

...it's that...
...es que...

...what some people call...
...lo que se llama...

Here he is, **back from the dead**!
*¡Uppaa, **llegó el desaparecido**!*

Careful with this one in the Southern Cone, where *los desaparecidos* refers to people who "disappeared" during various murder-happy dictatorships.

What the heck are you doing here?
¿Y tú, qué haces por aquí?

Great to see you!
¡Qué alegría verte!

You look great!
¡Qué pinta!

Where've you been hidin'?
¿Dónde te has metido?

You fell off the face of the earth.
Te esfumaste de la faz de la tierra.

Speak of the devil, **and he doth appear**.
*Hablando del Rey de Roma, **por la puerta asoma;...el burro se asoma**.*

This curious nickname for Satan actually dates back to the period of Papal exile in Avignon (1309–77), during which the "king" (technically Pontifice) of Rome was seen as a major heretic that the Church had to move to France to avoid. *Asomar* is a poetic botanical metaphor for "popping up" that conveniently rhymes with Roma; and *el burro* is the variation you use when you want to sneak in a jab at the intelligence of the Dark Prince in question.

You've put on a few [pounds] since the last time I saw you, Chubs!
¡Te engordaste un par [de kilos], Rechonchito!

Just when **we were too few**, and then...
*¡Tras que **éramos pocos**, y...*

For as clunky and sarcastic as it sounds in English, this is actually a fairly common, if folksy, way of announcing that you're happy to see someone.

> **Doofus** drops by!
> *cayó el **tronco**!*

> my brother hired a **drag queen**!
> *mi hermano trajo un **travesti**!*

> the **wild beast/the deaf girl/so-and-so** showed up!
> *llegó **la bestia/la sorda/fulano**!*

> **Granny** gave birth!
> *parió **la abuela**!*

> Don't ask me why this perverse spectacle would make for a kick-ass party... but it is somehow a common saying!

Hey!
¡Oye!

At some point, you'll probably need to catch someone's attention in a crowded street, open-air market, bar fight, or orgy. There are a bunch of ways to do so, but most are pretty regional—there's no universal "hey" aside from *oye* (listen) and *mira* (look), and even those have regional connotations (like in Argentina, where they sound more confrontational, like "listen up!").

Hey!

¡Oye! | *¡Aguas!* (Mex) | *¡Mare!* (Mex) | *¡Ala!* (Andes) | *¡Che!* (S.Cone)

Che is a trademark of the Argentine dialect, where it means both "hey" and "guy." Borges once "Argentinized" the story of Caesar and Brutus by substituting the famous "*et tu, Brutus*?" with an angry "*¡Pero, che!*"

Hey, man!

¡Quetá, compa!

Hey, now!

¡Épale!

Watch out!/Eeeasy there.

¡Eeeeeeh-pa!

Look!

¡Mira!

Listen!

¡Oye!

Listen up, deaf guy!

¡Oye, sordo! | *¡Oye, teniente!* (Spn)

Wake up, space-cadet!

¡Oye, ausente!; ¡Oye, zombi!

That's fucked up!

¡Qué mierda!

WOW!
¡CARAMBA!

If you want to sound like a hokey Ned Flanders anywhere in the Spanish-speaking world, then go ahead and use *caramba*. If not, here are some regional-specific alternatives.

¡Fua! (S.Cone)	*¡Caray!* (Andes)
¡Úchale! (Mex)	*¡Gua!* (Spanglish)
¡Diay! (CenAm)	*¡Hala!* (Spn)

Check this out!
¡Chéquele! | ¡Chécate esto! (Mex)

Check out that hairy guy's **back-bush!**
¡Cheque la barba dorsal que tiene ese gorila!

....

Seriously?
¿En serio?

What with all that subjunctive mood floating around, Spanish speakers tend to insist (and inquire) more often than English speakers about veracity.

No way!
¡No me digas!

Jesus Christ!
¡Cristo mío!

Holy shit!
¡Dio[s] mío!

I can't believe it!
¡No lo puedo creer!

Really?
¿De veras?

Are you for real?
¿Estás serio/a?

Give it to me straight.
¡Dime la dura! | ...la firme! (Peru) | *...la posta!* (S.Cone) | *...la fetén!* (Spn) | *...la neta!* (CenAm)

Yeah?
¿Sí?

You think?
¿Te parece?

Na-ah.
Ni modo.

Hell yeah!
¡Del todo!

Saying your goodbyes
Hacer las despedidas

Spanish farewells are a blank check for corniness. *Ciao*, the most common slang for "goodbye," is sometimes spelled phonetically, so don't be baffled by a *chau* or a *chao* on a billboard or in a comic book.

In a while, crocodile.
Chaufa. (Per)
This is a horrible Peruvian pun on Chinese food: *ciaofun*.

Lates!
¡Chabela!; ¡Chavela!
From *Ciao, bella*. *Ciao* is so common that many Latin Americans would be surprised if you told them it's actually Italian.

Bye, y'all.
Chado. (Col)
This is a pretty rural term.

See ya around!
¡Ahí nos vemos!

See ya in a bit!
¡Ahí nos vidrios!

I'm leaving.
Me voy.

Let's roll.
Larguémonos.

Let's get outta here.
Ahuéquemos el ala.

I gotta bounce.
Tengo que huir.

Take care!
¡Ciúdate!

We're outta here.
Nosotros nos huimos.

See ya later!
¡Hasta luego!

Toodles!
¡Ahí nos Belmont! (S.Am)
Belmont sounds like *vemos* (see ya) but is also the name of an ubiquitous brand of cheap Venezuelan cigarettes. Sounds Venezuelan, right?

Text me!
¡Mensajéame!; ¡Textéame!

Call me later!
¡Llámame luego!

L8R.
Elejota. (Chi)
The phonetic pronunciation of *L.J.*, which is the abbreviation for *los juimos*, Chilean slang for "Let's go."

Until next time!
¡Hasta la próxima!

Smell ya later!
¡Hasta el cante! (Spn) | *¡Hasta el hornazo!* (Mex) | *¡Hasta la chucha!* (Andes) | *¡Hasta la baranda!* (S.Cone)

Sorry
Sori

In Spanish, you don't so much apologize as plead distraction, momentary lapse of reason, ill luck, or simply general incompetence. Most Spanish speakers use self-deprecation to extract themselves from a sticky situation rather than beg forgiveness. So if you get caught cheating on your girlfriend or boyfriend, just say, "Whoops, aren't I the sillyhead!" and then grin until your cheeks hurt.

Sorry!
¡Perdón!; ¡Sorri!; ¡Sori!

I'm really, really sorry!
¡Lo siento muchísimo!

BLESSINGS AND GRACES
BENDICIONES Y GRACIAS

Catholicism is widespread in Latin America. And just as the British will say "Cheers" as you hand them an Alcoholics Anonymous pamphlet, many Spanish speakers will literally bless you even if you're wearing a giant star of David.

May God protect and keep you. (Formal)
Que Dios le proteja y cuide.

May God go with you. (Familiar)
Que vaya Dios contigo.

May God watch over you.
Que Dios te guarde.

I pray to God that my car won't fail me again.
***Ojalá que** no me falle el coche de nuevo.*
Fun fact: this phrase is actually borrowed from the Andalucian Arabic *law-sha-Allah,* or "if Allah wills it."

My bad.
Emece.
As in "M.C.": mea culpa.

Ooops!
¡Ufa!

It's totally my fault.
Tengo todo la culpa.

My deepest **apologies!**
¡Mil disculpas!

I crossed the line.
Me pasé de la raya.

Forgive me.
Perdóname.

I'm so embarrassed!
¡Qué vergüenza! | ¡Qué corte me da! (Spn)

What a stupid thing to do!
¡Qué idiotez!; ¡Qué huevada!

What a fuck-up!
¡Qué cagazón! (Mex) | *¡Qué boludez!* (S.Cone)

....

Get over it
Aguántatelo

If apologizing doesn't get you off the hook, you should move for a full dismissal of charges with appeals to a big picture or friendly license that might seem out of bounds in North American culture.

Let's not get carried away.
No es para tanto.

It's not what it looks like!
¡No es lo que parece!

I didn't mean to do that at all.
Lo hice sin querer para nada.

It was an honest mistake!
¡Fue sin querer!

I didn't mean to shit in your **bidet**!
*¡Cagué en tu **bidé** sin querer!*

Oh, don't **make a scene**!
*¡Ay, no **armes un escándolo**! | ¡Deja el show!* (PuR)

Take it easy.
Tómalo con calma. | Cógelo suave. (Carib)

Chill out, man, it's **just a dribble** of wine.
*Calma, hombre, es **un chorrito** de wine **nomás**.*

WHEN IN ROME...DON'T CALL THEM ROMANS
CUANDO VAYAS A ROMA, NO LES LLAMES ROMANOS

Know how people in New York like to call themselves New Yorkers and say they live in The City? Well, they stole that habit from Spanish speakers just like they stole Manhattan from the Indians. Here's a handy chart of the affectionate names Spanish speakers call themselves and their cities.

People who live in:	Call themselves:	And their city:
Buenos Aires	*Porteños*	*Baires, Buesas*
Madrid	*Madrileños, Gatos*	*El Foro*
Barcelona	*Barceloneses*	*Barna, Barça*
Mexico City	*Chilangos*	*El Monstruo*
Guadalajara	*Tapatíos*	*Guanatas*
Guatemala City	*Chapines*	*Guate*
Lima	*Limeños, Zapallos*	
El Salvador	*Guanacos*	
Nicaragua	*Nicas*	
Costa Rica	*Ticos*	

'Scuse me
'Miso

Latins don't have many ways of saying "excuse me." As the old saying goes, *mejor pedir perdón que pedir permiso* (better to ask for forgiveness than permission).

Excuse me.
Con permiso.

'Scus'ee.
Permiso.

Meepmeep!
'Miso-miso!

Make way, I'm in a rush.
Abre paso, *vengo apurado.*

Watch out!
¡Cuidado!

Back in a flash!
¡Vuelvo al tiro!

Please
Porfa

Spanish slang is supertheatrical. You'll often see adults pleading like children for a simple favor. That's because you don't merely ask someone for something; you paint them as your supreme benefactor, a noble gaucho who would forever be immortalized in song if they could somehow bring it upon themselves to pass the god-damn salt.

Pleeeeease!
¡Poorfaa!

Pretty please!
¡Plis-plis!

Please do me the favor.
Por favor, hágame el favor. | *...la gauchada.* (S.Cone) | *...la volada.* (CenAm)

I'm begging you!
¡Te lo ruego!

You scratch my back and I'll scratch yours.
¡Hazme un cambalache! | *...el cruce!* (Col)

Please have the decency to shut that gossiping mouth of yours.
Tenga la bondad de callar esa boca chismosa, por favor.

Help me out!
¡Échame una mano!

Can you do me a favor?
¿Me harías una cosita?

Good to meet ya
Un placer darte a conocer

After meeting someone, it's nice to express your pleasure at having done so. People like to be liked. Go figure.

I'm charmed.
Encantado.

Pleased to meet you.
Mucho gusto.
There's also the less formal *'chogusto.*

The pleasure is all mine.
El placer es todo mío.

Likewise.
Igualmente.

Have a good one.
Que te vaya bien.

Hopefully, we'll **bump into each other** again.
*A ver si **nos encontramos** por ahí.*

What do you do for fun?
¿Cómo te diviertes?

Once you've established that someone's gonna be at your table for a while and you've exhausted all small talk, it's far more acceptable than in the U.S. to press for personal details.

What do you do to kill the time?
¿Cómo matas las horas?

Where are your people from?
*¿De dónde viene **tu gente**?*
Here "your people" would refer to one's extended family or "kin," not to their race or ethnicity as in North American usage.

How long have you lived in the city?
¿Desde cuándo has vivido en la ciudad?

Where were you raised?
¿Dónde te criaste?

Can you show me around the city?
¿Me podrías pasear por la ciudad?

I don't know **anyone** here, can I sit with you?
*No conozco a **un alma** aquí, ¿podría sentarme contigo?*

Let's meet up later tonight, what do you say?
Nos juntemos a la tarde, ¿que te parece?

How single are you, exactly?
¿Cuán soltero estás, de hecho?

Where'd you learn **to open bottles** like that?
¿Dónde aprendiste descorchar botellas así?

Would you give me **a private lesson**?
¿Me darías una lección privada?

What team do you play for, if you don't mind my asking?
¿Para qué equipo juegas, si no te molesta la pregunta?

CHAPTER 2

Friends & Enemies
Amigos & Enemigos

The best way to internalize the rhythms of Spanish-speaking society is to watch *telenovelas* for a few hours a day and read some smutty comics. These pulpy media are a great way to sharpen your verbal and judgmental skills on fictional victims. They're also a good way to learn the codes of side-eye, shade, and the intricate webs of obligation and decorum undergirding social occasions in which people catch up and make new friends. This chapter will give you the vocabulary, but as with all things social, the real variation and nuance lies more in the context and the intonation.

Real friends
Amigotes

Spanish speakers have tons of words to describe their range of friends, many based on degrees of closeness. Even more so than usual, these terms vary not only from country to country, but also within countries, between classes, between cities, or even by neighborhood or social circle.

Best bud
Amigote/a

> He's my **best friend** from back in the day.
> *Es mi **amigote** desde hace mucho.* | *...**pana**...* (Carib)

Homie
Compinche | *Asere* (Carib)

BFF
Cuate (CenAm)

Homeboy
Esse (Spanglish)

Old school buddies
El/La cole (short for *colega*)

Roommate
Compañero de departamento
For someone who shares an apartment with you.

Roommate
Compañero de habitación
For someone who shares a room with you.

Roommate
Coinquilino
For that stranger you found on Craigslist.

My bro
Mi 'mano | *mi carnal* (Mex) | *mi pata* (Andes)

> How you been, **bro**?
> *¿Cómo viene la cosa, 'mano?*

My sis
Mi 'mana

> What's new, **sis**?
> *¿Qué hay de nuevo, 'mana?*

My boy
Mi compa'; Mi compai

> We've been **boys** forever.
> *Somos compas desde siempre.*

My girl
Mi comay

> Don't worry about her—she's **my girl**.
> *No te preocupes por ella—es **mi comay**.*

Drinking buddy
Compañebrio
Compañero (comrade) plus *ebrio* (drunk).

Dogg
Chavo (Mex)

Brah
Mijo/a
Although this is a term of endearment mothers use for their children, it can also be used as an affectionate, or more commonly, sarcastically affectionate, form of address between friends.

Peeps
Mi gente

Crew
La clica | el corillo (Carib)
Clica comes from the French *clique*. It means "gang," as in "the gang," or the more serious, "nowadays he's in a gang."

Posse
Aleros (CenAm)
Literally, "wingmen."

Bosom buddies
Amigos del alma

> They've been **bosom buddies** since they were little.
> *Han sido **amigos del alma** desde chicos.*

Duuuuuuude
Chavóoooon

As in any language, there are some names you say and others you just yell drunkenly across the bar at the end of the night. Here are the more affectionate ways to holler at your dude-bros.

Man!
¡Macho!

Dude!
¡Chavo! | *Parce* (Col)

Duuuuuuude!
¡Chavóooooon!

That guy
El tipo ese

Acquaintance
Conocido/a

Babe
Un/a buenote/a

Hunk
Un pibón (Spn)

Who's **that gal** you came with?
*Y **esa tipa** con la cual llegaste, ¿quién es?*

Chicky!
¡Chava!

Sweetheart!
¡Queriiido! (Arg)
This literally means "beloved," but somehow, even the manliest working-class Argies call each other this with no homoerotic connotation whatsoever.

Moms and pops
Mami y tata

Everyone's got a mother and a father. Unless you're an orphan, were born to gay parents, or were painfully abandoned as a child—in which case you can pretend your therapist is your *madre de leche*.

Daddy
Papi | Pai (Carib) | *Papay* (Andes)
In the mouth of an adult, *papi* often has the same nasty connotation that "daddy" would have in English, as in "Oooh, Daddy, don't stop!"

Dad
Papá | Apá (Mex)

Pops
El tata (LatAm) | *El taita* (Carib, Andes)

My old man/My old lady
Mi viejo/Mi vieja

A bad father
El pudre
This pun on *padre* literally means, "He rots."

Doofus dad
El tato
Tato literally connotes a stutterer with a hard-T speech impediment.

Mommy
Mamá; Amá (Mex) | *Mamay* (Andes)

Moms
Mami | Mai (Carib)

Stepmother (wicked or otherwise)
La madrastra
The suffix *-astra* means "secondary" (and implies "wicked") in many other family terms: *padrastro, abuelastra, hermanastro/a...*

Mother figure/adoptive mother
Madre de leche

You got momma's-boy-itis.
Tienes la mamitis.

Your mom!
¡La madre que te parió!

You talkin' about my mom?
¿Estás mentando a mi madre?

Other family members
Otros en la fami

Most nicknames for family members are pretty regional, but here are the universal basics.

You better get married quick if you don't want an **unrecognized son**.
*Tienes que casarte pronto si no quieres un **hijo natural**.*

The title of my honors thesis is "**Fatherless Sons**: The Legacy of Colonialism."
*El título de mi tesis de honores es "**Hijos espurios**: legados del colonialismo."*

Fidel Castro was the **bastard son** of a sugar planter.
*Fidel Castro fue el **hijo bastardo** de un hacendado de azúcar.* | *...**guacho**...* (S.Cone)

He thinks he's the **head of the household**, but his wife brings home the bacon.
*Él se piensa **padre de familia**, pero la esposa trae la lana.*

Man, your wife plays the **housewife**, but she couldn't bake you a *tres leches* to save her life.
*Ufa, tu mujer se viste bien de **madre de familia**, pero ni soñar que te haga un tres leches como la gente.*

That boy's one **apple that didn't fall far from the tree**.
*Ese chico **sí que salió hijo de su padre/madre**.*

Get out the rocker for **Gramps**.
*Traiga la mecedora para **el abue'**.* | *...**el yayo**.* (Spn) | *...**el nono**.* (S.Cone, from the Italian)

Your **gramma** is still kinda hot.
*Tu **abue'** sigue medio buena.* | *...**yaya**...* (Spn) | *...**nona**...* (S.Cone)

Easy there, **old-timer**.
*Con calma, **anciano/a**.* | *...**ruco/a**.* (Mex)

Booty calls
Consuelos sexuales

Most Spanish speakers don't think of sexual adventures as immoral or depraved unless they're jealous old schoolmarms addicted to *telenovelas*. And even when they do have something to say about shacking up, there's something tongue-in-cheek about their aspersions. These handy names for all the shades of gray between singledom and married life are less judgmental than their English equivalents. Don't be shocked to hear them used between people who don't know each other very well.

I gotta find me a....
Necesito encontrarme un/una....

> **boyfriend/girlfriend**
> *novio/a*
>
> **live-in boy/girlfriend**
> *arrejuntado/arrejuntada* | *juntada* (CenAm)
>
> **lover**
> *amante*
> *Amante* doesn't always imply sex, just intensity—so don't panic if someone says your 10-year-old sister has a lover!
>
> **companion/partner (domestic)**
> *'ñero/a*
>
> **special friend**
> *amigovio/amigovia* | *el/la jeva* (Carib)
> *Amigo + novio = amigovio.*
>
> **arm candy** (m. or f.)
> *el camote*
>
> **side-piece** (m. or f.)
> *segundo frente*

part-time lover
el tinieblo
As in, he sneaks in through the window and doesn't tell anybody about you.

friends with benefits
amigos con derecho

fuckbuddy
tragón/tragóna
This awesome word literally means "expert swallower" or "gulper." With a name like that, who *wouldn't* want a fuckbuddy?

booty call
un fijo/a

It's not serious, he's more of a **booty call** than anything.
*No es serio, él es más **un fijo** que nada.*

It's too early for that, we're still in **second gear.**
*Es temprano para eso, todavía estamos en **grado dos**; ...en **segunda**.*

You guys aren't even **shacking up** yet?
*¿Ustedes ni siquiera **se han arrejuntado**?*

Life of the party
El vacilón

Who we are as people and who we become in a space full of loud music, alcohol, and strangers are two very different things. Knowing your way around the flora and fauna of a party is just as crucial to language learning (and living a good life) as knowing how to navigate a crowded plaza, an office, and the DMV. Spanish-language parties are a blank check for melodrama, measured less by how many people are unsafe to drive, and more by the number of memorable scenes acted out.

What a drag!
¡Qué lata!

You are a/the...!
¡Eres un/una...!

He/She is (a)...!
¡Él/Ella es (un/una)...!

Quit being so/such a...!
¡No seas tan/un/una...!

> **life of the party**
> *vacilón/ona*
>
> **party animal**
> *calavera*
>
> **wallflower**
> *planchadora* (S.Cone) | *sujetacolumnas* (Spa)
>
> **party pooper**
> *aguafiestas*
>
> **buzzkill**
> *cortamambos*
>
> **wet blanket**
> *pinchaglobos*
>
> **freeloader**
> *aprovechado/a* | *piola* (S.Cone)
>
> **moocher**
> *remo*
> A *remo* is an oar—something that never pulls its own weight.
>
> **professional crasher**
> *paracaidista*
>
> **social butterfly/quick friend**
> *amiguero/a* (LatAm) | *macanudo/a* (S.Cone)
> Outside the Southern Cone, *macanudo* just means "upstanding" or "morally good."
>
> **out of it, in one's own world**
> *ensimismado/a*

sheltered nerd
nerdo | *zanahoria* (Andes) | *estafón* (PuR) | *zapallo* (S.Cone)

boring/wearisome
pesado/a | *pelma* (Spn)

conversational zero
lastre ("ballast"); *plomazo* ("lead")

formless blob
una plasta

Valium on legs
soporífico/a ("a sedative")

A real Eeyore
un/a bajanota

blowhard
fanfarrón/ona | *echón* (PuR)

real talker
picudo/a (Mex)

Class
Cuna

North Americans are sometimes shocked at how openly people in other countries talk about class. And class-talk is super common in Latin America and Spain, where there existed an honored aristocracy until quite recently (in many areas, the last names of the moneyed class still haven't changed). So don't be surprised when casual conversation takes a sudden turn for the socioeconomic.

He/She is so....
Él/Ella es tan....

bougie, precious
afectado/a | *cheto/a* (S.Cone)

basic
fresa/ón (Mex, CenAm) | *pijo/a* (Spn)

pretentious
agrandado/a; pituco/a (S.Cone, Andes)

fake
plástico/a

common
ordinario/a

tacky
cursi

trashy
jarca

stingy
codo
Literally, "elbow," as in, willing to put in a lot of elbow grease to save a drink.

fancy, showy
paquete

blue-blooded
de alcurnia | *de cuna* (S.Cone)

working-class
de plebe

top-notch
de categoría | *de catego* (Mex)

He's a total poser.
Con él, todo es pura pose.

How did that **tramp** manage to marry a doctor?
*¿Cómo llegó a casarse con un doctor esa **guarra**?*

She wishes she was **an A-list celebrity**.
*Ella sueña con ser **una de la farándula**.*

All those fashion designers in Mexico City are just **wannabe Euros**.
*Todos esos diseñadores de moda chilangos son **unos europizantes**.* | ...
unos malinchistas. (Mex)

Fun fact: La Malinche was the Aztec wife and translator of Hernán Cortés, and thus pivotal in the downfall of the Aztec Empire at Spanish hands, so it means a little more than "wannabe Euro"—think Uncle Tom.

I like **girls from good homes**.
*Por mi parte, yo prefiero a **las niñas bien**.*

....

Characters
Personajes

As in any language, there are certain terms that are used less to describe than to designate or typify. Every social circle (and every *telenovela*, at least by the second season) has at least one good specimen of each of the following:

Gossip
Chismoso/a

TAKING THEM DOWN A NOTCH
BAJÁNDOLES LOS HUMOS

Stuck up	*Fufurufo/a*
Bible-thumper	*Santurrón/Santurrona*
Gullible	*Palomo*
Crybaby	*Ñoño/a*
Lowlife	*Canalla*
Laughingstock	*Un/una hazmerreír*
Ex-con (literal or figurative)	*Reo/a*
Crass	*Grosero/a*
Brat	*Un/una niñato/a*
Bossy	*Mandón/Mandona*
A curmudgeon	*Un/una infeliz*
Pussy-whipped	*Un "siquerida"* (a "Yes, dear!")
Hermit	*Padre del yermo*
A decrepit old geezer	*Un vejestorio decrépito*

Snoop
Entremetido/a | *Metiche* (LatAm)
Meter means "to get into," as in, other people's business.

Small-town boy
Pueblerino/a

Hick
Paleto/a

Hippie
Hippy
Uninflected whether for men or women, plural or singular, noun or adjective—occasionally spelled *jipi*, but usually spelled the English way.

Good-for-nothing
Inútil

Slacker
Huevón/ona.

Bum
Vago

Badass
Gallito | *Chingón* (Mex)

Thug
Bruto

Twit/jackass
Capullo

Dork
Nerd; Nerdo

Geek, weirdo
Freaky
Sometimes spelled phonetically: *friqui.*

Fuck-up
Pato criollo (S.Cone) | *Gilipollas* (Spn)
The New World *pato criollo* (Muscovy duck) is, at least in folk wisdom, dumber than the European duck; even more graphically, *gil* (from the Latin *jill*) means

"dumb," and *pollas* "dicks" specifies what these dummies think with instead of their brains.

Slut
Culisuelta
Literally, "Loose ass."

Playboy
Mujeriego
Note, this morally neutral term can be used positively (ladies man) or negatively (womanizer), depending on the speaker's level of tolerance for machismo.

Skanks
Cueros

Some random dude
Un tipo cualquiera | *Un tío cualquiera* (Spn)

> She hooked up with **some random dude** last night.
> *Ella se enrolló con **un tipo cualquiera** anoche.*

Punk kid
Chamaco/a (Mex) | *Pibe/a* (S.Cone) | *Chaval/a* (Spn)

Don't get huffy, he's just a **punk kid**.
> *No te encabrones, es un **chamaco** nomás.*

A bastard
Un cabrón/ona (Mex)

> Your brother's a **real bastard**.
> *Tu hermano es **un cabronazo**.*

....

The gays
Los gay

The Hispanic world has queer scenes both underground and out in public. Since the turn of the millennium, LGBT tourism has boomed all over the tourist-friendly parts of Latin America, in many cases with sustained support from savvy local and federal governments (even in countries less accepting of their own LGBT communities).

Confusingly for the language learner, however, queer Spanish speakers often neutralize gay-bashing terms by using them affectionately, calling one another "Faggy" (*Marica*), for instance, just as flippantly as they might call each other "Fatty" (*Gordito*) or "Darky" (*Negrito*). But the effect is all in your tone, so make sure you use the following words like a sweetly smirking hostess serving at the dragbar, and not like some degenerate skinhead sulking out in front of it.

Since when does he/she dress like a…?
¿Desde cuándo se viste él/ella como…?

I don't care if everyone knows, I've always been a…
Qué sepan todos, siempre he sido…

>**flamer**
>*un mariposo; una loca*
>
>**nancy**
>*una mariposa*
>Literally, "a butterfly."
>
>**twink**
>*una mariquita*
>
>**femme**
>*un/una hembra*
>
>**cocksucker**
>*un mamahuevos; un chupapija*
>
>**butch**
>*una macho* | *una machona* (Andes, S.Cone) |
>*una machorra* (Mex)
>
>**bulldyke**
>*una marimacha; una machúa*
>
>**lesbo**
>*una tortillera* (Mex) | *una arepera* (Andes)
>Ever seen how tortillas and arepas are made by hand?

POLITICALLY INCORRECT
POLÍTICAMENTE INCORRECTO

Each culture's national and racial stereotypes tell us a lot about how they see the world, and they can be instructive to understand, even as they grow more and more taboo among younger generations.

Mexicanear
In a prison or criminal context, to snatch the heist from another thief or group of thieves; figuratively, to steal someone else's boyfriend or girlfriend right out from under them.

Hacer la uruguaya
A sleight-of-hand (or of tongue) at the cash register intended to get you more change than you're owed. Immortalized in the opening scene of international hit, *Nueve reinas* (2000).

Gitanear
Gitano, which means gypsy, leads to this expression meaning to smooth-talk, butter up, or scam. Also, to "gyp" someone...oh, wait.

Peruanear
In Southern Cone, also used as a synonym for *gitanear*.

Argentinear
To talk loudly and say nothing; to make an exuberant display of false erudition or plagiarized ideas. The author, it bears mention, is a proud Argentine.

Trabajar como un chino
It wasn't just in California that nineteenth-century Cantonese-speaking immigrants built the railroads and laundered the shirts—most of the Hispanic world got at least a few thousand able-bodied newcomers during those years and proceeded to give them the worst work they could find.

No hay moros en la costa
The coast is clear! This phrase dates back to Spain's religious wars to push the Catholic–Muslim boundary to Gibraltar, even though nowadays *moro* can refer to people of recent as well as distant African or Arab descent, depending on the context.

queen
una reina

drag queen
una travestí

He's totally **bent**.
*Es un **volteado** total.*

I bet she **plays for both teams**.
*Ella debe **jugar en las dos direcciones**.*

Manuel's **wifey** is a banker named Ezekiel.
*El **hembrito** de Manuel es un banquero que se llama Ezequiel.*

Lovey-dovey nicknames
Amoríficos

My baby
Mi amor

My better half
Mi media naranja

My sweetheart
Mi corazón

The apple of my eye
Alma de mi vida

My old man
Mi mareado (Mex)

My sweetie
Mi cariño

My old lady
Mi negra (Arg)

This term has, in most contexts, lost any (conscious) racial meaning it historically had.

Cutie (f.)
Mi bonbón

Dear
Mi querido/a

In Argentina, straight men have openly called each other this since Tango times—everywhere else, it's strictly for lovers.

Sweet talkin'
Galanteando

To flirt
Coquetear; Flirtear

To hit on
Ligar

To pick up
Levantar

Give me a holler.
Dame un toque; Dame un silbito.
Silbito means "a whistle."

Can I get your number?
¿Me darías tu número?

Can I buy you a drink?
¿Te compro algo para beber?

What are you doing tonight?
¿Tienes planes para la noche?

How was your date last night?
¿Cómo te fue la cita de anoche?

She is such a flirt.
Ella es una coqueta fatal.

Let's spend the night together.
¿Por qué no pasamos la noche juntos?

CHAPTER 3

Booze, Bars, & Clubs
Tragos, Bares, & Clubes

In all the lands where Spanish is spoken, despite stereotypes of *siestas* and nothing being open on Sundays, people work very long hours and take few days off. To offset the burden of this work ethic, Spanish speakers party at the drop of a hat—maybe not in the Anglo-American sense of the word (binge-drinking, shouting, and getting kicked out of places), but definitely in a more wholesome sense of the word (clowning, dancing, taking clothes off, etc.)

Where the party at?
¿Dónde hay pachanga?

I wanna...
Quiero...

> **go out tonight!**
> *salir esta noche!*

> **go big tonight.**
> *largar con todo esta noche.*

> **get some ass tonight.**
> *ligar esta noche.*

I think I'll just...
Me antoja más...

take it easy tonight.
pasarla tranqui esta noche.

stay home.
quedarme en casa.

hit the hay.
retirarme ya.

be a bum and watch TV.
hacerme el vago y quedarme con la tele.

hit the sack.
irme al sobre.

We should hit up that....
Debemos meternos en ese/esa....

Wanna crash a...?
¿Quieres colarte en un/una...?

> **house party**
> *pachanga* (Mex) | *jarana* (Spn)

> **block party**
> *festividad de barrio*

A TOTAL FREE-FOR-ALL
UN LÍO TOTAL

Here are terms for parties that require serious mopping-up or deep carpet cleaning, if not bail posting, afterward.

A huge blow-out
Un reventón

A first-rate megaparty
Un festejón de primera

A real riot
Un bochinche

A rager
Un bacanal

Utter chaos
Un barullo

No holds barred
Deschavetado (LatAm)

dance club
disco club (Spn) | *boliche* (S.Cone, Andes)

dive bar
antro barato (Mex)

fun little shindig among friends
party; pari

little party in someone's apartment
fiestita depto

backyard BBQ
asado; barbacoa (Carib) | *parrilla* (S.Cone)

ranch party
fiesta ranchera; fiesta de quinta (more upscale)

These are massive ragers where everyone crashes in the many bedrooms of a family's ranch house or timeshare—without concern for neighbors or cops—for days on end.

high roller party
fiesta paquete

masquerade
baile de máscaras

These haven't died out just yet, although they mostly just happen in bordellos nowadays.

Too broke to go out
Me quedo por misio

There aren't a lot of valid excuses to turn down an invitation when your friends invite you out—or at least, not a lot of quickly accepted ones. You can expect a lot of haggling and nagging if you say you have work or an early morning or an obligation to your significant other, etc. The only quick way out of the invite is to be flat broke. Gear up with a slangy way of declaring it, and have an illustrative example ready of just *how* broke you are; it's just the fastest way. Or, if they're real friends and really want you to go out anyways, it might even backfire—and you don't pay for a thing all night!

I don't have **the dough**.
No tengo la lana; ...el pan | ...la pasta (Spn) | *...la guita.* (S.Cone)

I'm flat **broke**.
Estoy misio | chiro. (Ecu)

I am pretty **strapped**.
Estoy pelado | a dos velas. (Spn)

We're **hard-up**.
Estamos tiesos | en la olla. (Col)

I don't have **a buck to my name**.
No tengo ni un duro | ni un clavo. (Spn)

He hasn't got **a pot to piss in**.
Él ni tiene dónde caerse muerto.

Having fun?
¿Divertiéndote?

An important part of taking someone out is checking in and taking measurements on the fun-o-meter. Here's some vocab for barometric and temperature readings.

You **having fun**?
¿Estás disfrutando?

> **Yeah, this place doesn't suck.**
> *Wow, genial, este lugar.*
> Wow, pronounced flatly enough, is clearly sarcastic even through the worst accent.
>
> This little hole in the wall is really **bumpin'**!
> *¡Este rinconcito está a toda madre!* (Mex)
>
> I feel like **cutting loose**.
> *Me da por vacilar.*

Check out all these **hotties**!
*¡Mírale a estas **chavelitas**!*

This place is **super chill**.
*El lugar está **rebueno**.*

Let's go...!
¡Vámonos...!

> **hit on some girls/some guys**
> *a ligarnos unas chicas/unos chavos* (LatAm) | *unos tiós* (Spn)

> **get a drink**
> *a echar un trago*

> **get our groove on**
> *a soltar una juerga*

> **get stupid**
> *a deschavetarnos* (LatAm)

> **home**
> *a casa*

> **somewhere else**
> *a otra parte*

> **get the fuck outta here**
> *lejos de esta mierda*

I'm **really digging** what the DJ is spinning.
*Estoy **gozando mucho** lo que está tocando el DJ.*

Check it out, your friend's really **getting down**!
*¡Éjele, que tu amigo está **vacilando**!*

Yeah, she's **grinding all over** that guy.
*Sí, ella le está **haciendo un buen perreo**.*

This place is seriously **a dive**!
*En serio que este lugar es **un tugurio**.*
Literally, "a shepherd's hut."

Yeah man, **it blows**.
*Simón, **es una mierda**.*

Let's get out of this **shithole**.
*Larguémonos de este **pedorreo**.*

Let's bounce.
Huímonos.

....

Cheers
Salud

As part of Europe, Spain has a culture of hard drinking similar to our Anglo-American one. Social interactions are often well-lubricated, complete with drinking songs and games. In Latin America, however, binge drinking is seen as more pathetic or self-destructive than social or funny, and having one too many isn't usually something to brag about the way it is in American frat culture.

Let's go for **a drink**.
*Vámonos para **un trago**. | ...**un chupo**.* (S.Cone)

Wanna **knock back a few**?
*¿Quieres **echar unas copas**? | ...**unos copetes**?* (Chi)

> **Cheers! A toast!**
> *¡Salud! ¡Brindis!*
>
> **To good friends!**
> *¡Brindemos por los amigotes!*
>
> **To Pancho Villa, and his rebel 'stache!**
> *¡A Pancho Villa, y su bigote bandido!*
>
> **Bottoms up!**
> *¡Arriba, abajo, al centro, pa' adentro!*
> Say the words to this mock-ceremonial toast as you move your glass high (*arriba*), low (*abajo*), toward the center (*al centro*), and then down the hatch in one quick gulp.

Customer service can be incomparably more casual in a Spanish restaurant than in its Latin American equivalent, and nowhere more so than in bars, where a bartender might even address you as "shorty" or "wise guy." It's just one more way that the culture of alcohol is far less universal than decades of advertising would have you believe.

KEEPING IT POSITIVE
BUENAONDEANDO

Words for "cool" can be pretty localized, but here are some all-purpose adjectives for being stoked and stoking others:

Guay (Spn)	*Bárbaro* (S.Cone)
Pípiris (Mex/US)	*Maza* (LatAm)
Copado (S.Cone)	*Mola* (Spn)
Padre (Mex)	*Genial* (S.Cone)
Chévere (Carib)	*Chido* (Mex)

What'll it be?
¿Qué quieres? (Spn)

What can I get you, sir?
¿Qué le puedo servir al señor? (LatAm)

Gimme....
Dame....

> **a beer**
> *una cerveza | una caña* (Spn)
>
> **a brewskie**
> *una chela* (LatAm) | *una birra* (S.Cone, Andes) |
> *una cheve* (Mex)
>
> **a cheap beer**
> *una cerveza barata*
>
> **a third-rate beer**
> *una cerveza de tercera*

a beer on tap
una cerveza tirada

a bottle of beer
una botella de cerveza

a shot
un trago corto | un traguito chupito (Spn) |
un caballito (Mex)

a glass of wine
una copa de vino

Let's pound these shots.
Tráguemonos estos traguitos.

Hey, bartender, **a round** for my friends.
*Oye, camarero, **una ronda** para mis amigos.*

Chug! Chug! Chug!
¡Traga! ¡Traga! ¡Traga!

Bottoms up!
¡Al fondo!

What beers do you have **on tap**?
*¿Qué cervezas **tiradas** tienen?; ...**de barril**...*
Tirar is the verb for pulling the tap, so draft drinks are "pulled" drinks.

Shitty beer
Cervezuela
The suffix *-uelo/a* is a condescending diminutive, ranging in severity from
"humble" to "off-brand" to "shitty."

Watery beer
Cervezagua

Let's pop some **bubbly** to that!
*¡Adelante con **las burbujas**!*

Champagne
Champán; Champaña

Girly drink
Una bebida de nenas

Cocktail
Cóctel; Cubata
Cubata was once slang for *cuba libre*, but now it's slang for any mixed drink.

Hard liquor
Aguardientes

With so many gloriously fermentable ingredients at their disposal, Spanish speakers have a plethora of specialty drinks that they can make like no others.

Tequila

Made from the blue agave or *maguey* cactus, tequila has been central to Mexican drunkenness since pre-Columbian times, when drinking *pulque* (an undistilled form you can still get in some rural areas) was a sacred and often hallucinogenic way of worshiping *Mayáhuel*, the goddess of rowdiness, fertility, and peeing yourself in public.

Mezcal

Jalisco may have a trademark on *tequila*, but old-school Oaxaca's got its own variation: the *pulque*-like and earthy *mezcal*, in which swims the larva of the famous *hypopta agavis* worm. In spite of this wiggly deterrent, *mezcal* has gotten so trendy in recent years that in 2017, the *New York Times* reported an international shortage as demand surged.

Daquirí

OK, maybe you think daquiris are tacky. But hey, in climates where fresh, ripe fruit is dirt-cheap and available year-round, it belongs in your cocktail.

Cuba Libre!

Be careful with this one; the name comes from the revolution *before* The Revolution, so you might wanna call it a *ron con coca y lima* if you're actually in Cuba ordering this with Communist Party members around.

Telegrama

If you like mint but think mojitos and juleps are too sweet, maybe you'll like this rum and crème de menthe on ice.

Calambuco

A Cuban moonshine rum—though you might not wanna get too adventurous with drinks that could *blind* you.

Chicha

This is a general category of Andean corn-based drinks, usually but not always fermented and alcoholic. In Peru, old women sometimes start the fermentation process by chewing on the corn and spitting it out. Mmmmmm, nothing beats old lady spit!

Pisco Sour

Peru's famous distilled brandy *pisco* is mysteriously mellowed out when you add it to whipped raw egg whites, simple syrup, a dash of bitters, and the juice of a very acidic Peruvian lime.

Sangría

Many of Spain's full-bodied wines are fierce, vinegary, and cheap. That's why adding melty ice, sweet fruits (like apples), and a tart middleman like blood-orange juice isn't just a good idea; it's a national treasure.

Michelada

Mexico has always been home to a plethora of seafood-alcohol combos, but no one would've expected a mix of cheap beer and canned clam juice to become the international hit it has, leading to the odd state of affairs in which gas stations all across North America serve canned clam-beers to a mix of diasporic Mexicans, truckers, and people who have vacationed in clam-beer country.

PARTY ALL WEEK!
SEMANALCOHÓLICA

Gluglunes	Glug-glug-glug
Mamartes	Mamas, you suck like a baby on a mammary.
Miercolitros	Liters and liters of the stuff
Juevebes	And you drink.
Beviernes	And you drink, all week, and on the weekend...
Sabadrink	Let's have a drink!
Dormingo	Sleep it off!

Canelazo

It gets real cold in the Andes, every night, for much of the year, so hot toddies are a crowd-pleaser from Bogotá to Tierra del Fuego. The most common, cinnamon-forward of these is made with whole sticks, orange slices, brown sugar, and a dangerous amount of *aguardiente* or *caña*.

Vodka
Vodka

Whiskey
Whisky

Gin
Ginebra

Rum
Ron

Their drinks are **watered down**.
*Las bebidas ahí vienen **aguadas**.*

This is some **cheap tequila**.
*¡Qué **tequililla**!*

I'll have a whiskey with a beer **chaser**.
*Dame una whisky con un **remate** de cerveza.*

Drunkenness
Borrachera

Try extra hard to memorize these phrases. By the time you actually need them, there's no way in hell you'll be able to pull out this book and look 'em up.

I'm....
Estoy....

Americans love to get....
A los norteamericans les encanta ponerse....

> **drunk**
> *borracho/a* | *cuete* (Mex)

buzzed
achispadito/a

tipsy
choborra
Scrambling syllables makes it cutesy and adds a wink-wink connotation, in this case conveying more affection and less judgment than *borracho*. It's not more or less drunk, it's just less pathetic.

well-done
cocido/a (S.Cone, Spn)

shitfaced
mamado/a | *doblado* (Spn)

sloppy drunk
picado/a; taja (Spn)
Literally, "minced" or "chopped."

pickled
curado/a

wasted
fumigado/a (Mex) | *punto* (Spn)

We were drinking everything in sight.
Nos chupamos hasta el agua del inodoro.
Literally, "we drank everything...including the toilet water."

Last night we all **got totally trashed**.
*Anoche todos **nos pusimos pedos**.* (LatAm) | *...**se agarró un pedo**.* (S.Cone)
Pedo literally means "fart," and anything done *al pedo* is done pointlessly or blindly.

Last night we **went on a binge**.
*Anoche **fuimos de juerga**.* | *...**de cuete**.* (Mex)

I can't even remember **driving drunk**.
*Ni siquiera me acuerdo haber **conducido cuete*** (Mex) | *...**manejado moña**.* (Spn)

Sounds like a serious **bender**.
*Suena como **un vinagre** serio.* (Spn) | *...**una curda**...* (S.Cone)

That fool is such a/an....
Ese gil es un...total.

> **lush**
> *beodo*

> **happy drunk**
> *happy*

> **alkie**
> *borrachín*

> **boozer**
> *bebedor/a | chuzo* (Spn)

The morning after
La mañana siguiente

Of course, all this cirrhosis-inducing drunkenness has its consequences.

I'm about to....
Estoy a punto de....

> **throw up**
> *largar*

> **puke**
> *buitrear* (CenAm, Andes, S.Cone)

> **projectile vomit**
> *lanzar*

> **pass out**
> *desmayarme*

I have a **splitting hangover.**
*Tengo una **cruda aguda.**; ...un **guayabo agudo.*** (Andes)
The latter literally means "severe guava tree."

He's/She's **hungover.**
*Él/Ella está **crudo/a.*** (CenAm) | ...***chuchaqui.*** (Andes)

I got mean **dry-mouth** today.
*Hoy tengo una **secona** feroz.*

Something's banging around in my head.
Tengo un ratón en la cabeza.

I got so drunk last night I **pissed the bed**.
*Me emborraché tanto anoche que **me meé la cama**.*

Did we fool around last night?
¿Echamos algo anoche?

I don't remember dick about last night.
De anoche no me acuerdo un carajo.

I feel like shit.
Me siento como la mierda.

I gotta sleep off this buzz.
Necesito dormir la mona.

I've got the spins.
Estoy todo mareado.
As in, I just got off a boat after a shaky day on the open *mar*.

I'm so nauseous, man.
Estoy todo descompuesto, compa'.

I'm never drinking again.
Nunca más voy a tocar bebida.

Cancer sticks
Tubitos de cáncer

Tobacco may be persecuted in the First World, but when you stray off the beaten path in the tourist-loving Third World, you'll find that vast swaths of the population give zero fucks about secondhand smoke—since, you know, they have other problems to worry about, like famine and guerrilla warfare and whatnot. Whether you love the stuff or want cigarettes eradicated from all public places, here are the terms you'll need to know to get in or out of that cancer-cloud.

You smoke?
¿Fumas?

You gotta light?
¿Tienes fuego?

You sell **smokes**?
*¿Vendes **zafiros**?* (Mex)

Can you spare a **cig**?
*¿Te sobra un **faso**?* (S.Cone)

Can I bum a **cigarette**?
*¿Te puedo deber un **tabaco**?*

Not a single **cancer stick**?
*¿Ni un **cáncer**?*

Just one **drag**!
*¡Una **calada** nomás!* | *un **plon*** (Andes) | *un **toque*** (S.Cone)

Not even from the **butt**?
*¿Ni siquiera del **pucho**?; colilla*

Can I use your **lighter**?
*¿Me prestes un **encendedor**?* | ***mechero*** (Spn)

You're a fiend. You must **smoke like a chimney**.
*Eres un maniático. Debes **fumar como una chimenea**.*

Yeah, **I chain-smoke** like a whore in the slammer.
*Sí, **fumo uno tras otro** como puta encarcelada.*

Could you stop **exhaling in my direction**?
*¿Podrías parar de **soplar por aquí**?*

I'm trying to quit.
Quiero dejarlo.

Marijuana
Marejuancho

Spanish speakers have thousands of variants (mostly very local/specific ones) for talking about Mary Jane, from *mare-juancho* ("makes-Johnny-dizzy") to *mariguano* to *marihuan* to *mora* ("berry," the cutesy variant of the Mexican *mota,* and for berry kushes in particular). In many rural areas of Latin America, particularly in the vast majority of Latin American climates in which it literally grows like a weed, marijuana use is tolerated despite being illegal. In fact, in many areas, smoking more than the occasional toke might be grounds for a ribbing but hardly for concern or prosecution; in other areas, however, it can be a mortal sin or a serious offense. As always, feel out the situation with an eye to social class and your own position as an outsider before jumping to any conclusions.

Weed
Mota (Mex)

Bud
La marimba (Andes)

Herb
La hierba; La hierbabuena

Hash
La grifa | *El costo* (Spn)

> I'm feeling all **hashed out**.
> *Me siento **grifo** del todo.*

Wanna smoke **a joint**?
*¿Quiéres fumarte **un pito**?*
Pito also means "tube" and "rod," so you can imagine the double entendres.

Let's roll a **fatty**.
*Dale, hagámonos un **porro gordito**.*

When are we gonna roll that **spliff**?
*¿Cuándo vamos a liar ese **canuto**?*

Toke that **roach**!
*¡Tóquete ese **puchito**! | ...**bacha**! (Mex)*

Should we **hotbox it**?
*¿Debemos **hornearlo**?*

I'm so **high**, dude.
*Estoy tan **fumadito**, huevón.*

Man, do I love **smokin' dope**.
*Como me gusta **fumetear**.*

You look **nicely baked**.
*Te ves **bien arrebata'o**. (Carib)*

I only took one **hit**!
*¡Solo tomé un **toque**!*

Nah, I'm just a bit **lightheaded**.
*Nada, es un toque de **la pálida**.*

Whatever, you're a **pothead**.
*Ni modo, eres un/una **fumero/a**.*

At least I'm not a **burnout**.
*Por lo menos no soy un/una **quemado/a**. (S.Cone)*

I gotta hit up my **dealer**.
*Necesito pegarle una llamada al **vendedor**. | ...**vendemota**. (Mex)*

I got a mad case of the munchies.
Estoy mariguantojando. | ...motantojando. (Mex)
This is a portmanteau of *mariguana* and *antojando*, "craving."

Doped up
Puesto

Although much of America's hard drugs come from Latin America, using the hard stuff is pretty rare in the developing world, and none too openly discussed either, given the steep penalties for possession in *any* quantity. Still, here's some handy slang for substances people use to sully the temples of their bodies, in case you find yourself backstage.

Snort a bump.
Jalar un toquito.

Where can I score some...?
¿Dónde puedo conseguirme...?

> **pills**
> *pastis* | *chocho* (Mex)
>
> **blow**
> *perica* (LatAm) | *blanquita* (Andes) | *frula* (Arg) | *merca* (S.Cone) | *farlopa* (Spn)
>
> **snow**
> *nieve*
>
> **powder**
> *talco*
> As in talcum powder.
>
> **high-octane coke**
> *mosca* (Mex)
>
> **rock**
> *piedra basuco* (Andes)
>
> **a bag of "white" (coke)**
> *una bolsita de "blanquito"*
>
> **ecstasy**
> *éxtasis* (Mex) | *tacha* (Mex) | *rola* (Carib)
>
> **Xanax**
> *palitroques*
>
> **heroin**
> *el caballo jaco* (Spn) | *chiva* (Mex)
> Also known as horse.

> **gram bag**
> *una grapa* (Mex)
>
> **dime bag**
> *un pase* (Col)

Coked up
Empericado (LatAm)

You ain't nothing but a...
No eres más que un/una...

> **cokehead**
> *angurri* | *enfarlopado/a* (Spn)
>
> **horsehead**
> *yonqui* (Spn)
>
> **dope fiend**
> *drogata*
>
> **junky**
> *tecato/a* (Mex) | *falopero/a* (S.Cone) | *jincho/a* (Spn)

They just went to the bathroom to **do lines**.
*Se fueron al baño a **jalar rayas**.*

He's sweating like that 'cuz he's **kicking**.
*Suda así por **la malilla**.* (CenAm) | *...**el mono**.* (Spn)

THE SHANTYTOWNS
BARRIOS PERDIDOS

When you're searching for a good nightclub, you might want to avoid straying into Latin American shantytowns, which tend to be druglord-controlled autonomous zones way off the utility and police grids. For all the exoticism, though, they are home to their own non-governmental utilities, police forces, real estate markets, and everything else—shadow cities which, in some cases, might even house more residents than the legal ones. For a practical introduction, see Robert Neuwirth's *Shadow Cities.*

That shit must be good cuz that boy is **trippin'**.
*Debe ser bueno eso porque ese chico está **volando**.* | *...**del otro lado**.* (Carib, Spn)

You are **tweaking**, bro!
*¡Estás **volando**, mano!*

Don't drink that beer! I think that scumbag tried **to roofie** you.
*¡No tomes esa cerveza! Me parece que ese reo intentó **emburundangarte**.*

Houses of ill repute
Casas libertinas

Prostitution, though technically illegal, is alive and well in Latin America, and by comparison to puritanical North America, fairly open and above ground. Even if you're not planning on hitting up any brothels in your travels, you should know the terminology so you can avoid being taken there by well-meaning hosts. In fact, since these terms are often jokingly used to refer to a parties or social events with lots of eligible singles, this vocab comes up surprisingly often.

Who wants to go to a **cabaret**?
*¿Quién quiere ir a un **cabaré**?*
A cabaret is a like a burlsesque or dance hall.

> Sure, as long as it's not a **crab-eret**.
> *Bueno, con que no sea un **cabarute**.*
> These don't have stages or dance floors; instead, they're straight-up brothels.

Could we compromise on a **gentlemen's club**?
*¿Y si transijamos en una **casa de idolatría**?*

> Fine, let's roll to the **titty bar**.
> *Vale, larguémonos al **antro de vicio**.*

Me too, I'm down for an [American-style] **strip club**, but let's skip the **brothel after-party**.
*Yo también, estoy dispuesto a un **estripclub**, pero no **el after** en un **burdel**.*

Seriously, I got crabs at the last **whorehouse**.
*En serio, me tocaron ladillas en la última **ramería**.*

Man, that's because that nasty place was a **flophouse**.
*Chavón, es porque ese lugar asqueroso era una **chinchería**. | ... **piringundín**. (S.Cone)*

How much for an hour?
¿Cuánto la hora?

Prostitute
Pelandusca

Hooker
Puta

Street walker
Lumia (LatAm) | *Lumiasca* (Spn) | *Yira* (S.Cone)

Pimp
Proxeneta

Madame
La señora

Stripper
Encuerista | *Encueratriz* (Mex)

Don't be a snitch!
¡No seas soplón!

Unless your idea of tourism involves seeing the inside of a Third World prison (not recommended), you may wanna study up on these important bywords for police presence.

Here come the...!
¡Viene/Vienen...!

po-po
la pole

billyclubs
las cachiporras | *las lumas* (S.Cone)

cops
la cana | *la tomba* (Andes)

fuzz
los pacos (LatAm) | *la jura* (Mex)

pigs
los cuicos (Mex) | *los puercos* (Carib) | *los cobanis* (S.Cone) | *los bolillos* (Col)

Fuck the police!
¡A la mierda con la pole!

It wasn't me, I swear!
¡Yo no fui, lo juro!

Hide your **stash!**
*¡Esconde el **clavo!*** (Mex) | *...la **clatera!*** (Andes)

Oh shit, they're using the **billy clubs!**
*¡Mierda, están usando las **porras!*** | *...los **bolillos!*** (Andes, S.Cone)

They're gonna put us all in **lockup!**
*¡Nos van a meter todos **en la chirola!***

Damn, they **nabbed** Pookie and took him away **in cuffs.**
Agarraron** a Pookie y se lo llevaron **engrillado.

He's gonna end up in **the joint.**
*Va a terminar en **el bote.***

Well, he best remember that **snitches get stitches.**
*Le convendría acordarse que **los batidores salen bien batidos.*** (S.Cone)

CHAPTER 4

Sexy Body, Ugly Body
Cuerpo Cuero, Cuerpo Feo

Hey, Fatso!
¡Oye, Gordo!

Spanish speakers are pretty blunt when describing each other's physical characteristics. Someone with a big beard is called Beardy, someone shaped like a pear is called Pear. A well-hung man is called...You get the point.

Hey...!
¡Oye...!

> **bignose**
> *narigón/ona*

> **flatnose**
> *chato/a; ñata*
> This latter term often carries a potentially racist connotation of having native blood.

> **manga eyes**
> *focojos*
> Literally, "spotlight."

> **one-eye**
> *tuerto/a*
> To say "look the other way" in Spanish, you'd say *se hace tuerto*, which is pretty funny if you think about it.

one-arm
manco/a
Saying *no es manco* ("he's not one-armed") about someone means they're handy.

baldy (with a shaved head)
pelado/a

baldy (male-pattern)
calvito
From *calvo*, "skull."

baldy
pelón de hospicio
This is bald "like a hospital patient."

bighead
coco grande

egghead
cocudo
Literally, "coconut to spare."

bushybeard
barbudo

Mick Jagger mouth
jetón/ona

thick lips
hocicón

fatlips
bembón/ona (LatAm)
Bembón can refer to puffy or pillowy lips, but it can also refer to phenotypically West African lips as well—so be careful not to use the term in a racializing or racist way!

bigass
nalgón/ona

bigtits
pechona | *chichuda* (Mex)

birthin' hips
caderota

fatbelly
panzón/ona

old saggy (f.)
adelcaida

dwarf/little guy
petiso

midget
enano/a

short stack
chato/a
Careful when using this one—it implies stockiness, not just compactness!

big, bulky dude
grandote

gym rat
tiarrona/tiarrón

giant
gigante

beanpole
langaruto

toothpick
tílico/a | fifiriche (CenAm)
This refers to someone who looks not just skinny, but unhealthy.

The whole package
El paquete entero

Here are the standards to describe the people who float your boat. When traveling, be sure to pay attention to local terms for hot men and women, because every region of every Spanish-speaking country has its own unique words. A lot are based on local food vocabulary—*una torta, una manteca, un churro, un chile, una chilera...*

He/She....
Él/Ella....

> **is fine**
> *es fina*
>
> **is adorable**
> *es preciosa*
>
> **is gorgeous**
> *es espléndida*
>
> **will make you drool**
> *es para babearse*
>
> **will leave you speechless**
> *te deja atónito*
>
> **is very sexy**
> *es bien sexy*
>
> **is hot shit**
> *es lo más*
>
> **is in shape**
> *está cuajado/a* (Col)

That girl **is hot**.
*Esa chica **está buena**. | ...**es maciza**.* (Spn)

She's a **stone fox**.
*Es una **buenota**.*

Your mom's a **ten**, buddy.
*Tu vieja es **un cuero**, macho.*

Your sister's a **cutie**.
*Tu hermana es un **bizcocho**.* (Mex)

Is it weird to think that Steve Urkel is **a total hunk**?
*¿Es raro pensar que Steve Urkel es **un buenón total**?*

What a **hottie**!
*¡Que **cuerazo**!*

Ohmigod, there are, like, so many **hot guys** here.
*¡Epa, mira los tantos **papis** que hay por aquí! | ...**papuchos**...* (Mex)

I love men with **big guns**.
*Como quiero a los hombres con **brazos macizos**.*

Your little brother is **ripped**!
*¡Tu hermanito está **fornido**! | **cachas***

Her arms are so **toned**, it's pretty hot.
*Sus brazos están tan **marcados**, es bien rico.; ...**bien cortados**...*

Damn, he is **so cut**!
*¡Ufa, que está **bien dado**! | ...**manga**!* (Col) *| ...**calote**!* (Mex)

Lookin' **slim**!
*¡Te ves **delgado/a**!*

Are you a swimmer? You've got a **solid build**.
*¿Nadas? Tienes un **buen lomo**.*

Ugh, I am so **out of shape** these days.
*Pe', estoy tan **cuajado** en estos tiempos.*
Literally, *cuajar* means to congeal, like when curds becomes cheese.

He's **gone soft around the middle**, bigtime.
*Él **se volvió un flan**, pero mal.*

My girl's/guy's got....
Mi novi' tiene....

> **a good figure**
> *una buena figura | un buen lomo* (S.Cone)
>
> **a bangin' body**
> *un cuerpazo*
>
> **a hot bod**
> *un cuerpo estelar*
>
> **a narrow waist**
> *una cintura ancha*

an hourglass figure
un cuerpo de guitarra
Literally, "a body of a guitar."

nice legs
buenas gambas
The old East Coast slang, "gams," comes from the same Italian word.

gorgeous eyes
ojos deslumbrantes

big doe eyes
ojotes de coneja

Fugly
Defeorme

Because sometimes you just gotta tell it like it is.

The thing is, he's just **fucking ugly**.
*Lo que tiene, es que es **feo como la mierda**.*

Damn! **She's heinous!**
*¡Carajo! ¡Es **atroz**!*

Is it just me, or is Mary Kate kind of **formless**?
*¿Es cosa mía, o es Mary Kate un poco **amorfa**?*

> At least she's not **frumpy**.
> *Por lo menos no es **babosa**.*
> Literally, a "slug."

Dude, your dad is so **hairy**!
*Hombre, ¡que **peludo** es tu viejo!*

He's a little **chubby in the cheeks** for my tastes.
*Para mí, él es un poco **fofito en las mejillas**.*

What've you been eating, **tubby**?
*¿Qué estás comiendo, **fofo/a**?*

What a **lardass**!
*¡Qué **gordinflón/ona!** | ...**pamplón/ona!** (Carib)*

> Hey, don't start with me, **Pillsbury**.
> *Epa, no te metas conmigo, **Michelin**.*

I have a **major double chin** in this pic.
*Tengo **una papada real** en esta foto.*

Ugh, you want me to talk to that **hunchback**?
*Ufa, ¿quieres que hable yo con ese/a **jorobado/a**?*

Were you born **bowlegged**?
*¿Naciste **rengo/a**?*

Sorry, but she's not skinny, she's **skeletal**.
*Disculpe, pero ella no está flaca, está **esquelética**.*

You look like an **emaciated** P.O.W.
*Pareces un/a prisionero/a **enclenque**.*

Did you see that **mug**?
*¿Viste a esa **careta**? | ...**caripela**? (S.Cone)*

Check out **four-eyes**.
*Mírale **cuatro ojos**. | ...**piticiego**. (Chi)*

It's sad he has such a **Pinocchio nose**.
*Es una lástima **la cayuya** que tiene. (Chi) | ...**tocha**... (Spn) | ...**napia**... (S.Cone)*

Hey, **gaptooth**!
*¡Oye, **chimuelo!** (Mex, CenAm)*

Stylin'
Engalaneado

What good is your slammin' body if you're dressed in a sack and haven't changed your drawers in six days? Here are some handy phrases for describing the stylish—or not quite stylish, as the case may be.

He/She looks....
Él/Ella se ve....

> **fashionable**
> *galano/a*
>
> **put-together**
> *bien compuesto/a*
>
> **O.C.D.**
> *T.O.C. (trastorno obsesivo-compulsivo)*
> As in, your shoelaces match your belt, bag, underwear, and eyeshadow.
>
> **well-groomed**
> *prolijito/a*
>
> **unkempt**
> *descuidado/a*
>
> **sloppy**
> *desaliñado/a*
>
> **threadbare**
> *deshilachado/a*
>
> **like a real mess**
> *bien abandonado/a*

Tits and ass
Tetas y culo

The Eskimos, it's said, developed over 100 words for snow because they've been surrounded by the terrible, freezing stuff every moment of their miserable lives. Ergo, Spanish speakers must be up to their ears in sweet, delicious ass because they have more ways to describe booty than the ancient Greeks had gods.

You have a great **bust**.
*Tienes un **delantero** tremendo.*

Play with my....
Juega con mis....

You have beautiful....
Tienes unos/unas...hermosas.

Could I motorboat your...?
¿Puedo hacer trompetillas con tus...? (Mex)

> **breasts**
> *senos*
>
> **boobies**
> *bubis*
>
> **knockers**
> *globos*
>
> **titties**
> *chichis* (Mex)
>
> **tits**
> *tetas* (Andes) | *lolas* (S.Cone)
>
> **hooters**
> *gemelas* (Col)

She's got some perky little breasts, doesn't she?
¿Tiene pechugitas paraditas, no?

You could ski jump off those little peaks.
Podrías hacer salto con esquis en esas respingonas.

She's bursting with personal endowments.
Ella tiene una pechonalidad tremenda.

Does she have fake boobies?
¿Tiene las teclas falsas?

She is so flat-chested, she looks like she hasn't even hit puberty yet.
Ella tiene el pecho tan liso que parece ni entrada en pubertad.

Those are some saggy boobs.
Están bien caidas esas tetas.

Those are just ugly boobs.
Esas son pechufeas.

She has enormous nipples.
Ella tiene pezones enormes.

His nipples are kind of weird.
Él tiene las tetillas algo raras.

I'm in love with your....
Estoy enamorado de tu/tus....

> **derriere**
> *trasero*
>
> **butt**
> *fondillo*
>
> **bottom**
> *poto* (Andes)
>
> **butt cheeks**
> *nalgas*
>
> **heinie**
> *pompis* (Mex)
>
> **ass**
> *culo* | *traste* (S.Cone)
>
> **fat ass**
> *culón*
>
> **ass crack**
> *raya del culo*
>
> **ass cheeks**
> *ancas*
>
> **buns of steel**
> *ancotas de plomo*
>
> **firm glutes**
> *tambo* (CenAm)
> Tight like the head of a drum (*tambo*).

Look how she shakes that money maker!
*¡Mira como mueve el **cubilete**!*

Damn! Check out that **big-booty girl** with all that junk in the trunk!
*¡Pucha! ¡Mírale todo el cargo que lleva esa **nalgona**!*

Your boyfriend is **totally assless**.
*Tu novio es **totalmente desnalgado**.*

I love Latinas and their **thunderbutts**.
*Como me gustan las latinas con esas **ancotas temibles** que llevan.*

I prefer British girls with those **right-solid rumps**.
*A mí me da más por las inglesas, con esas **ancas bien sólidas**.*

I tell ya, I just can't with those **superflat butts**.
*Te digo, no puedo con esos **fundillos de aspirina**.*
Ever looked at an aspirin pill?

Spare tires
Llantas

People come in all shapes and sizes. Some are tall, others are compact. Some work religiously to maintain nice, tight abs. Others with busier schedules and more carb-heavy diets have stomachs that spill over their jeans like overyeasted dough. Far from English speakers' impersonal and medicalized approach to discussing the bodies of others to mask implicit or private judgments, Spanish speakers are quicker to speak in familiar terms, use food metaphors and diminuitives, and make their agendas and preferences quite explicit, the way one might talk about a sibling or a lover in English. Try not to look shocked if you're trying to blend in!

You sure have a soft **belly**.
*Tienes la **panza** muy suavecita.*

Man, your dad's really got a **beer gut**.
*¡Qué **guata** tiene tu viejo, hombre!* (S.Cone, Andes) | *...**botijón**...* (CenAm)

Is that woman actually with child, or is she just **gigantic**?
*¿Esa mujer está con hijo de verdad, o tiene el **bombo** nomás?*

You gotta start working off that **spare tire**.
*Deberías liberarte de esa **llanta**.* (LatAm)

What about your **muffin-top**?
*¿Y tu **bollito**?*
Bollo (bun) also has a lot of local usages: "turd" in Colombia, "dyke" in Spain, "vulva" in Cuba...

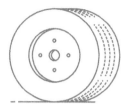

Nice **six-pack**! Do you work out?
*¡Linda **tabla de chocolate**! ¿Haces ejercicios?*

> Nah, these **washboard abs** just come natural.
> *Psh, esta **tabla de lavar** vino así.*

Piss and shit
Pis y mierda

Like most bodily functions in the Spanish-speaking world, the acts of peeing and pooping aren't considered scandalous enough to generate much eloquence or circumlocution, unless you're trying to be cutesy or jokey. If you are, though, there are any number of quaint metaphors you can deploy for comic effect.

I gotta....
Necesito....

> **hit the john**
> *irme al trono*
>
> **drain the lizard**
> *achicar la verga*
> Note that the Spanish word doesn't actually mean lizard, so don't go pointing out any *vergas* at the zoo.
>
> **tinkle**
> *hacer pipí | hacer chichi* (Col) | *puchar* (S.Cone)
>
> **take a piss**
> *mear*

HITTING THE LOO
VISITAR A LA ROCA

In addition to the many standard, general terms you might have learned in Spanish class (*el servicio, el lavatorio, el baño...*) you might also hear in your travels a good number of slangier terms with subtle differences of meaning.

Full bathroom
Los higiénicos
This type of bathroom would maybe include dressing rooms, a well-lit makeup sink, the works.

Washroom
El lavabo; El aseo
This room might not have a toilet but definitely has a mirror behind the sink.

Washroom sink
La cubeta; El lavamanos

Basic/minimal bathroom
El excusado
This bathroom probably has a squat toilet, and maybe a sink.

The toilet
Inódoro
This can refer to the appliance itself or the room, but in the latter case it's about as vulgar as it would be in English.

Shitter
El trono

That bathroom is cleaner than my **bidet** at home.
*Esa tina es más limpia que el **bidé** en mi casa.*

Sorry, **latrine**'s out of order, bud.
*Perdón, **la letrina** está discompuesta, chico.*

That **crapper** is disgusting, I'll hold it for now.
*Ese **retrete** es un asquete, me lo guardo por ahora.*

mark some territory
poner la firma

take a shit
cagar

drop a **turd**
*depositar un **zurullo** | ...**sorete** (S.Cone)*

drop off a **dung delivery**
*echar una **entrega de estiércol***

I....
Yo....

>   **am constipated**
>   *estoy estreñido*
>
>   **have diarrhea**
>   *tengo una cursera; tengo churras*
>
>   **have the shits**
>   *tengo la cagadera*
>
>   **have the runs**
>   *tengo un chorrillo* (Mex) | *estoy de carreritas* (Carib)
>
>   **left skid marks on my drawers**
>   *dejé un sello en los calzones*

I got drunk and **pissed myself**.
*Me emborraché hasta **mearme** todo.*

Wake up, before you **wet the bed**.
*Despiértate antes que **te mees en la cama**.*

I'd wait a while before you go in there. I just dropped **a deuce**.
*Yo por tí esperaría un cacho. Acabo de hacer **el dos**.* (Mex)

It smells awful. **Did you shit yourself?**
*¡Qué aliento! **¿Te cagaste?***

Bodily fluids
Fluidos corporales

Spanish speakers don't actually have much slang for bodily fluids.
They're kind of nonchalant about them.

Earwax
Cerilla

Unplug your ears, jackass!
*¡**Sácate las velas de las orejas**, gil!*

Snot
Moco

> I have a terrible **runny nose**.
> *Tengo una **moquera** terrible.*

> He **got the snot knocked out of him** in that accident.
> ***Se hizo moco** en ese accidente.*

Wipe off your **eye boogers**, you mouth breather!
*¡Quítate las **legañas**, baboso!*

Your **pimples** are getting out of control.
*Tus **espinillas** se están desbordando.*

> You need to **pop those zits** before your face explodes.
> *Tienes que **apretarte esos granos** antes de que te explote la cara. | ...* ***barros**... (Carib)*

> Everyone **gets blackheads** now and then.
> *A todos **nos salen granitos** de vez en cuando.*

Is that **drool**?
*¿Son **babas**?*

> Don't **drool all over yourself**, that's my sister!
> *¡No **te babees todo**, esa es mi hermana!*

Spit it out, it's nasty!
*¡**Escúpelo**, está asqueroso!*

To menstruate
Menstruar | Reglar (Mex)

> I have **menstrual cramps**.
> *Tengo **los cólicos**.*

> Her **monthly visitor** came.
> *Le vino **la regla**.*

> **Aunt Flo** is visiting.
> ***Don Goyo** está de visitas. (Carib)*

Don't start with her, she's **on the rag** somethin' fierce.
*No metas pata, está **monstruando** bien serio.*

Do you have an extra **tampon**?
*¿Te sobra un **tampón**?*

All they have are **pads** in this damned country!
*¡En este maldito país no hay mas que **toallitas**!*

Other bodily functions
Otras funciones corporales

Damn you just **ripped** one!
*¡Carajo, acabas de **largar** uno!*

That's OK, I'll return fire with a loud **tooter**.
*Está bien, te devuelvo fuego con un **cuete**.* (LatAm)

Sorry, I just let out a **silent but deadly**.
*Disculpe, acabo de **zurrar**.* (S.Cone)
Outside of the Southern Cone, this refers to involuntary incontinence.

I'm terribly gassy.
Estoy con un gas tremendo.

Uhhhh! Who **farted**?
*¿Uuuuu, quién se **cuescó**?* (Spn)

I bet I can **burp** louder than you.
*Te apuesto que **eructo** más fuerte que tú.*

Dude, you've got some rank **B.O.**
*Hombre, tienes un **grajo** que espanta.* (CenAm, Carib) | *...una **baranda**...*
(S.Cone) | *...un **cante**...* (Spn)

How's my **breath**?
*¿Cómo está mi **aliento**?*

Saying my dad **snores** is an understatement; he's a sawmill!
*Decir que mi viejo **ronca** sería quedarse corto; ¡es un aserradero!*

I used to **grind my teeth** in my sleep.
*Antes **rechinaba los dientes** cuando dormía.*

Stand me up, I'm all **dizzy** from smoking so much pot.
*Párame, que estoy todo **mareado** de tanto fumetear.*

She's **preggers**.
*Está **encinta**.*

Her degenerate of a boyfriend **knocked her up**.
*El degenerado de su novio **la empreñó**.*

He put some bread in her oven.
Él le llenó la cocina de humo.
Literally, "He filled her kitchen with smoke."

Did you take a **home pregnancy test**?
*Hiciste la **prueba de embarazo casera**?*

Ailments
Achaques

If you're a true traveler to Latin America, you'll encounter plenty
of spicy food, hard liquor, outdoor plumbing, and disease-carrying
mosquitoes. Add 'em all up and chances are you're gonna get sick.
But it all makes for a better story when you get home, so stop your
sniveling, and eat the worm already!

I feel awful.
Me siento pésimo.

I feel like **total crap**.
*Me siento como el **culo** | ...el **orto**. (S.Am)*

He is very ill.
Él está muy mal.

I have a **migraine**, get me a **painkiller**!
*¡Tengo **jaqueca**, alcánzame un **calmante**!*

I'm so nauseous.
Tengo nauseas tan fuertes.

Move, I'm gonna...!
¡Muévete, que voy a...!

> **throw up**
> *echar buitre* (LatAm)

> **puke**
> *trallar*

> **hurl**
> *guasquear* (Andes) | *huacarear* (Mex)

How did I end up **covered in vomit**?
*¿Cómo terminé **cubierto en vómito**?*

He'll be **praying to the porcelain goddess** all night.
*Va a pasarse la noche **devolviendo atenciones**.*
Literally, "writing thank-you cards."

I think I got **scabies** from sleeping in that creep's bed!
*¡Me parece que me tocó **la sarna** durmiendo en la cama de ese reo!*

I have **stomach cramps** from eating all that meat.
*Tengo **retortijones** por comer tanta carne.*

He's got **a bit of a gimpy leg**, right?
*Tiene **la pierna medio coja**, ¿verdad?*

> Is he still **walking with a limp**?
> *¿Sigue **cojeando**?*

Do you wanna see my **bruises**?
*¿Quieres ver mis **moretones**?*

Those are **bite marks**!
*¡Esos son **mordiscos**!*

I need some....
Necesito....

> **strong drugs**
> *drogas fuertes*

> **Ibuprofen**
> *Ibuprofeno*

Tylenol
Tylenol

laxatives
laxantes

barbiturates
barbitúricos

CHAPTER 5

Nice & Naughty
Dulzuras & Travesuras

Despite what Americans might presume about a Catholic-led public sphere, sexual expression is wide out in the open in the Spanish-speaking world, as ubiquitous as advertising is in America. Newsstands sell hardcore porno next to kids' comics, websites proudly rank the best sexual catcalls, and TV newscasters are often as sexualized and dolled up as Vegas showgirls doing a Dolly Parton routine. While this can make public space seem hostile or barbaric to people coming from Protestant or Islamic cultures, where sex is more of a private matter, having so much dirty laundry and hijinks out in the open also lowers the stakes of moral judgment somehow. Spanish speakers have "natural," not illegitimate, children; they tell "green" jokes instead of dirty ones; they become "green" old men instead of dirty old ones; and they have extramarital "adventures" instead of affairs. But like so many things in Hispanophone culture, the theory and the practice, or more precisely, the institutions and the daily life, are worlds apart—consider, for instance, that in a majority of Spanish-speaking countries, divorce and abortion have only been legal for a generation, and in some of them, they still aren't.

Fucking 101
Coger 101

There is no universal Spanish term for fucking. Spaniards use *joder* and Mexicans use *chingar,* both of which mean "to fuck" in those countries but "to irritate" everywhere else. The rest of Latin America uses *coger.* But Spaniards never got the memo and still use *coger* in its dictionary sense of "to catch, get, or hold." This causes mass hysteria among Latin Americans whenever they hear a Spaniard talking about needing to fuck a bus. To add to the confusion, *trincar* has the opposite problem and means "to seize or grab" everywhere except for Spain, where it means "to fuck." You might wanna draw yourself a little chart at the airport and avoid all these terms on layovers.

I wanna....
Quiero....

Do you want to...?
¿Quieres...?

Let's go and....
Vámonos a....

I'd love to....
Me gustaría....

> **have sex**
> *tener sexo*
>
> **fuck**
> *coger | chingar* (Mex)
>
> **bang**
> *culear | fifar* (S.Cone)
>
> **screw**
> *tirar | follar* (Spn)
>
> **boink**
> *curtir* (S.Cone)

knob
empomar

hit that
comérsela

bone
joder

Joder, like the British "bugger," can mean anything from mild, nagging irritation to sodomy. Most of the time it hovers ambiguously in between.

plug her
enchufarla (Mex)

knead that dough
darle masa (Andes)

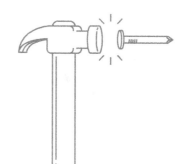

nail that ass
clavar ese culo

have a fuck
echar un palo

have a double-fuck
echar un doble-palo

have a fuckathon
echar un buen caldo

Ever made broth (*caldo*) from scratch? It takes all day.

have a quickie
echar un rapidín; un cuiqui

leave it raw
fregarla; cepillarla

Fregarla is literally, "to scrub it," while cepillarla translates as "to scrub it with a cleaning brush."

hook up
ligar

pick someone up
levantarle a alguien

get involved with someone (sexually)
meterse con alguien

Gettin' horny
Arrechándose

A word should capture the essence of the thing it stands for—and for some reason, sex occasions as much onomatopoeia as babies or puppies. This general global truism isn't the case in English, however, where even in the 21st century, most of our sex vocabulary is made up of excruciating Greek or Latin medical terms like "ejaculate" and "climax" that turn sex into some kind of science fair project. Modern-day Spanish, on the other hand, uses lyrical, poetic phrases like "boil over," "outdo yourself," and "go into a frenzy" that capture a little more of the chaos and fun of sex, without the gauze and curtains. It is anything but sterile.

Damn, girl, you're getting me **all excited**.
*Ufa, chica, me estás dando **un buen morbo**.* (Spn)

You make me so **horny**.
*Me pones tan **arrecho/a**.* (LatAm) | *...**bellaco/a**.* (Carib)

I've got **a boner that won't quit**.
*Tengo **un duro que dura**.*

I'm **hard** for you.
*Estoy **al palo** para ti.*

I'm **ready to go**.
*Estoy **a full**.*

I want it **inside me**.
*Lo quiero **adentro**.*

Why don't we **do it** right here?
*¿**Por qué no lo echámos** aquí nomás?*

Tell me how you want it.
Dime cómo lo quieres.

Oh, you **feel so good.**
Ooo, estás bueno.

You're **so big and hard.**
*Estás **tan duro y grandón**.*

Wow, you're **really wet** today.
*¡Wow, qué estás **bien húmeda** hoy!*

You're **gettin' me hot and bothered!**
*¡Me estás **calentando la estufa**!*
Literally, "stoking the stove."

Come on, **faster! Harder!**
*¡Dale, **más rápido**! ¡**Más duro**!*

Are you close to **cumming?**
*¿Estás por **correrte**? ; ...**venirte**?*
Literally, "to run, flow, or brim over."

Fuck, I'm gonna **cum!**
*¡Carajo, me estoy por **llegar**!*

Cum on my face.
***Lechéame** la cara.*

BURY THE BONE
HUNDIR EL HUESO

Freír la berenjena	Deep-fry the eggplant
Engrasar la nutria	Grease the marmot
Enhebrar el hilo	Thread the needle (i.e., anally)
Enterrar la batata	Bury the yam
Medir el aceite	Dunk the dipstick
Revolver el estofado	Stir the coals
Serruchar el piso	Saw the floor
Peinar para adentro	Comb it from the inside
Ñaca-ñaca	Hubba-hubba
Frike-frike	Freaky-freaky
Dunga-dunga	Humpy-humpy

Do it, then.
Hazlo, pues.

Oh yeah, **take it all**, you freak!
*¡Ja, **tómalo todo,** loca!*

Other sex acts
Otros actos sexuales

The best way to learn Spanish is by immersion and exploration, figuring things out as you go—particularly in your personal life. I strongly recommend dating someone who prefers Spanish and avoids English when you talk to them, even avoids English in the very explanations of what you don't understand about Spanish. Sex vocabulary, however, probably fits squarely in that special list of exceptional words you want to already know inside and out before the first time you encounter them in the field, lest you mistakenly agree to do something you will regret. You might want to dog-ear this page and review it often before going on any dates that might end well, or badly, or sloppily, or...well, you get the idea.

Will you suck me off?
¿Me lo chuparías?

Wanna **blow me**?
*¿Quisieras **mamármelo**?*

I like it when **you swallow** my cum.
*Me gusta cuando me **tragas** la leche.*

I want you **to ride me** like a pony.
*Quiero que **me cabalgues** como una yegua.*

C'mon, just give me **the tip**.
*Dale, dame un **puntazo** nomás.*

If you don't have a condom, just **jizz** all over me.
*Si no hay condones, **dispárame en blanco** nomás.*

Pull out at the last minute and **splash it on** my tits.
*Al fin, **ponla en marcha atrás** y **salpícame** las tetas.*

I'd like to try....
Quisiera probar....

How 'bout...?
¿Qué tal...?

Have you ever done...?
¿Has hecho alguna vez...?

> **dry-humping**
> *la frottage* (from the French)

> **a blow job**
> *una mamada; un pete* (S.Cone)

> **a full-service blow job**
> *recitar el rosario*

> **a hand job**
> *la paja* (LatAm)
> Literally, "tumbleweed."

> **a circle jerk**
> *una carrera de pajas* (LatAm)
> Literally, "jackoff race."

> **a circle suck**
> *una margarita*

> **a threesome**
> *un trío sexual*

> **an orgy**
> *una orgía*

> **a sex party**
> *el partus; una "fiesta"*

> **69**
> *sesenta y nueve*

breast wank
la paja rusa

anal sex
sexo anal

backdoor action
la trastienda
Literally, "backdoor dealings."

cunnilingus
el buceo
Literally, "diving."

a snowball
un beso blanco

a rim job
un beso negro

the ol' finger in the butt
la espada de Carlomagno
Isn't "Sword of Charlemagne" more fun to say than "finger in the butt"?

a golden shower
una lluvia dorada

WHAT'S YOUR FAVORITE POSITION?
¿CUÁL ES TU POSICIÓN FAVORITA?

Missionary	*Misionero*
Doggy-style	*La adoración; El perrito*
Cowgirl	*Cabalgando*
Wheelbarrow	*La gran carretilla*
Standing T	*El cartero* ("the postman")
Spoon	*En caja*
Reverse cowgirl	*Cabalgando hacia atrás*
Both knees up	*La defensa amorosa*
Both legs up	*El candelabro*
Ankles on giver's shoulders	*Los abdominales* (an abs workout!)
Knees held spread	*El barco de vela* ("the galley")
Spoonee turned halfway back	*La santanderina*

I'm sick of...let's fuck already.
Estoy harto de...quiero coger ya.

Why the rush to bang? First I wanna (do some)...
¿Por qué tanto apuro a coger? Antes quiero...

> **making out**
> *enrollarnos* (Spn) | *bregarnos* (Carib)
>
> **foreplay**
> *cachondear* | *fajar* (Mex)
>
> **cuddling**
> *franelear* (S.Cone)
>
> **third base**
> *darnos el lote*
>
> **pawing at each other**
> *magrearnos*
>
> **finger you**
> *dedearte; darte dedo*

Nuts and bolts
Tornillos y tuercas

Unless you're gonna be a doctor, you should probably expand your selection of sex nouns beyond the medical ones you learned in school. I wish there were space to convey the astounding richness of regional and poetic variations, but alas, a guide is not the same as an encyclopedia, which is what we'd end up with if I tried to include all the thousands of Spanish names for "junk."

Grab my....
Agárrame....

Play with my....
Manotéame....

Suck my....
Chúpame....

Touch my....
Tócame....

You have (a) huge....
Tienes muy grande(s)....

> **privates**
> *los agentes*
>
> **member**
> *el miembro | el socio* (Andes)
>
> **package**
> *el paquete; el bulto*
>
> **nuts**
> *las bolas | los belines* (S.Cone)
>
> **balls**
> *los huevos | los cojones* (Mex)
>
> **ball sac**
> *las talegas* (CenAm) | *las pelotas* (S.Cone)

DICK-TALK
JERGA VERGA

Tree trunk	*El tronco*
Soup can	*El marlo* (literally, "corncob")
One-eyed giant	*El chino tuerto* ("slanted eye" = urethra)
Baldy	*El pelado*
The hose	*La manguera*
The meat stick	*La butifarra, morcilla*
The stick shift	*La palanca*
Piece	*El pedazo*
Knob	*El pomo*
Limp dick	*Un pene de soga*
Micropenis	*El cacahuete; El maní* (literally, "peanut")

boner
la puntada

dick
el pito

cock
la verga | el bicho (PuR)

mast
la asta

rod
el pijo; la pija (S.Cone) | *la polla* (Spn)

shaft
la pinga | la poronga (S.Cone)

prick
el pincho

weiner
el nabo; la pirula

Uncut
Con pellejo | Con forro (Carib) | *Encapuchado* (S.Cone)

Jizz
Leche; Güasca | Lefa (Spn)

....

'Gina talk
Chochisme

Lick my....
Lámeme....

Hit my....
Méchame....

Eat my....
Cómete....

Shave my....
Aféitame....

> **pussy**
> *la chocha* | *la crica* (Carib)
>
> **pooch**
> *el potorro* (Spn) | *la pucha* (Mex) | *la pusa* (CenAm)
>
> **twat**
> *la chucha* | *la cuca* (CenAm)
>
> **pussy lips**
> *el bollo* (Carib)
>
> **carpet**
> *la alfombrita; el felpudo* ("the felted bit")
>
> **bush**
> *el arbusto; la selvita* ("the little jungle")
>
> **box**
> *la pandorca* (Carib)
>
> **peach**
> *la castaña*
> Literally, "chestnut."
>
> **beaver**
> *el sapo*
> Literally, "toad."
>
> **clam**
> *la almeja*
>
> **cooch**
> *la concha* ("conch shell") (S.Cone) | *la panocha* (Carib)
>
> **cunt**
> *el funciete* (Mex) | *el coño* (Spn) | *la tota* (Carib)
> Spaniards also use *coño* as an expletive like "fuck!" or "shit!"

shaved pussy
la chocha afeitadita | *la chocha rasurada* (Mex) | *la concha rapada*
(S.Cone)

clit
la campana ("bell"); *el botón* ("the button")

G-spot
el punto G

cameltoe
el hachazo

perineum
el periné

Accessories
Accesorios

Nowadays, you can't really call yourself worldly if you don't know your way around a sex shop. They all sell pretty much the same things everywhere, made in the same Chinese factories. And why would you be reading this book if you didn't want to be more worldly? Even if you're not comfortable with or interested in using any of these 21st century gadgets and sanitary barriers, it never hurts to know what they're called, if only for the sake of puns and double entendres!

Are you on **the pill**?
¿Estás tomando la píldora?

Man, I miss my ex, who had an **IUD**.
Como echo a menos a la ex que tenía "DIU."; ...la "T.";...el ancla.
El ancla is literally, "the anchor."

Do you have...?
¿Tienes...?

> **a condom**
> *un preservativo*

a rubber
un impermeable | un forro (S.Cone)

any piercings
perforaciones

an STD
una venérea
You can also use this to call someone "a walking STD."

handcuffs
las esposas | las chachas (CenAm)

Shit! The **condom** broke!
*¡Mierda, se quebró el **forro**!*

Reach me a...
Alcánzame un/una...

Wanna try a...?
¿Quisieras probar con un/una...?

I love using a....
Me encanta usar....

> **dildo**
> *un consolador*
> *Consolador* literally means "consolation," like for not having the D on hand when you want it.
>
> **vibrator**
> *un vibrador*
>
> **blindfold**
> *una venda*
>
> **tickling cockring**
> *un párpado de carba*
> This glorious phrase literally denotes the eyelashes of a goat. Isn't Spanish beautiful?
>
> **gag**
> *una mordaza*

paddle
una pala

Sexual sociology
La sociología sexual

Sadly, double-standards around sexual expression and morality are a long way from vanquished anywhere in the world. The Spanish-speaking world still shows fear and shame at female promiscuity. But as a proud Latin American, I hope this is another false impression created by the vast chasm between strict moral traditions and a more empathetic way of navigating social life day in and day out. Just in case I'm justified in my optimism, don't assume when you hear these pejoratives and epithets that the speaker is endorsing them genuinely—there is lots of room here for camp, irony, histrionics, and playfulness.

That **horndog** would fuck anything on legs.
*Esa **cachonda** cojería cualquier cosa con piernas.*
Literally, "bitch in heat."

Too bad he's an **impotent**.
*Qué lástima que es un **deficiente sexual**.*

That **sterile dude** couldn't even get you pregnant with the love of God.
*Ese **huevo duro** no te podría impregnar ni con el amor de Dios.*

Eww, you **pervert**!
*¡Bua, **perverso**!*

She keeps cheating on her **cuckold** of a husband.
*Ella le sigue engañando al **cornudo** de su marido.*
This is one of the most common and severe insults in Hispanic culture. It means you've been cheated on and made a fool of, and is frequently insinuated by making the devil horns sign with your hand and bumping it against your temple.

Stop **making a cuckold of** my brother!
*¡Basta de **ponerle los cuernos a** mi hermano!*

Careful, he's **a ladies' man** and **a swinger** to boot.
*Ojo, que es **un mujeriego** y en cima **un partusero**.*

He's always **sleeping around**.
*Siempre **anda culeando**.*

He may be cute, but that guy is a total **manwhore**.
*Está bien churro pero es un **perrote** total.*

You'll never get your rocks off with that **dicktease**.
*Nunca vas a echar un polvo con esa **calientapijas**.*

Your girlfriend is **frigid**.
*Tu novia es una **chuchafría**. (Andes) | ...**coñofrío**. (Spn)*

That **easy slut**'s got a **quick-action pussy**.
*Esa **culopronto** tiene una **concha de lata**.*

Yes, *concha de lata* does mean "aluminum pussy." Why? Because aluminum gets hot in seconds flat, that's why.

I wouldn't date **a loose girl** like her.
*Yo no me metería con **una flojona** como ella. |*
*...**una conchuda**... (S.Cone)*

I tend to go for **cougars**.
*Yo suelo andar tras las **asaltacamas**.*

She looks like **a virgin**, but I think she just **plays innocent**.
*Ella se parece **invicta** pero yo pienso que **se hace la inocente** nomás.*

Jerking off
Pajas y pajeros

The most common and universal term for male masturbation, *paja*, is also the word for tumbleweed, which rolls around the plains in its eternal circular motion—poetic, huh? A *pajero*, then, can mean a drifter (like Don Quixote, for instance); it could feasibly refer to a hay-monger; and in some places it means someone who babbles an endless stream of unimportant small talk. But nine times out of ten, it means an excessive self-lover. In 1983, Mitsubishi even tried marketing an SUV to Latin America's quixotic drifter types under the name Pajero, but their dismal sales returns showed that no one wanted to drive around with "wanker" written on their car. Here are some less poetic synonyms if you want to avoid repeating Mitsubishi's gaff.

They call him the **King of Jacks**.
*A él le dicen **el Rey de la Paja***.

He's a chronic **wanker**.
*Él es un **puñetero** mordaz*.

He never stops **choking the chicken**.
*Nunca se cansa de **pelársela***.

He's always asking for help **wacking off**.
*Siempre pide ayuda **haciéndose una chaqueta***. (Mex)

I usually **rub one out** before I go to bed.
*Suelo **cascarme una pajita** antes de dormir*.

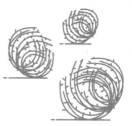

CHAPTER 6

Smack Talk
Las Fanfarronadas

Cursing in Hispanic cultures is a hugely popular, over-the-top form of poetry. Friends spar against each other like mortal enemies, gossips interrupt their narratives to unleash bucolic torrents of abuse on innocent passersby, and taxi drivers with little hope of a tip will spend five whole minutes roundly cursing a fellow driver. It's a way of life, a whole grammar of embellishment, and a popcorn-worthy public spectacle that isn't uncommon for strangers to drop everything to watch. Study up, or you might never fit in.

Pissed off
Encabronado

Latins aren't more hot-blooded than other peoples, they're just more open and expressive about life's little murderous rages and *cabrón* ("billy goat") incidents.

Fucking wetback beaners....
Frijoleros mojados....
Google the music video *Frijolero*, by Mexican rock supergroup Molotov, to get a feel for just how offensive this term is in either language.

Heartless, deportation-crazed Republicans....
Republicanos deportadores despiadados....

Euro-style mullets....
Esas melenas de gallego fofo (LatAm).... | *Esas melenas de futbolista sudaca* (Spn)....

> **make me angry**
> *me enojan*

> **tick me off**
> *me ponen del hígado*

> **piss me off**
> *me encabronan*

> **get on my nerves**
> *me ponen de los nervios*

> **really bother me**
> *me molestan seriamente*

> **annoy the hell out of me**
> *me fastidian hasta la madre*
> Etymologies differ, but for many, your nerve has your mother's name written on it.

You better not **piss me off**!
¡Mejor que no me chingues! (Mex)

Shut up!
¡Cállate!

Shut your trap!
¡Cierra el hocico!

You talk a lot of **bullshit**.
*Tú dices mucha **mierda**. | ...**paja**.* (CenAm)

Get the hell away from me!
¡Pírate, carajo!

Get outta my face!
¡Lárgate de aquí!

I've fuckin' **had it** with you!
*¡Me tienes **harto**!*

SWEARING
PUTEANDO

Here are some expletives to shout out when you hit your thumb with a hammer, in order of severity from "gee-willikers" to "&#^%$!" Note that most of the weaker terms are catachreses (deliberate mix-ups for near-sounding words) of the severe terms, as in any language.

Shucks!	¡Barajo! (Carib)
Shoot!	¡Miércoles!
Frickin' A!	¡Chuta! (S.Am)
Darn!	¡Jolines! (Spn)
Nuts!	¡Pucha!
Son of a...!	¡Hijue'!
Damn!	¡Joder! (Spn)
Balls!	¡Chuca!
Shitty!	¡Caray!
Shitballs!	¡Carajo!
Fuck!	¡Puta!
Motherfucker!	¡La puta madre!
Goddamotherfucker!	¡La gran puuuta!

Leave me alone.
Déjame en paz.

I'm about to lose my shit.
Estoy perdiendo mi puto quicio.

Now we're really up shit creek without a paddle.
Ahora sí que estamos con la mierda hasta el cuello.

Keep cussin' me out and I'm gonna snap any second.
Sigue puteándome y en cualquier momento voy a soltar la rabia.
Somehow, "unleash the fury" (*soltar la rabia*) sounds less hokey in Spanish.

Eat a dick!
¡Vete a la verga!

Go fuck yourself!
¡Vete a la mierda! | ¡Vete a la chingada! (Mex)

You talkin' to me?
¿A mí me lo dices?

What's your problem, man?
Pero, ¿qué te pasa?

What're you on about?
¿De qué vas?

What the fuck are you looking at?
¿Qué mierda miras así?

Don't front!
¡No vaciles! (Spn) | *¡No bolacees!* (S.Cone)

What the hell is going on here?
¿Qué demonios está pasando por aquí?

What the fuck do you want, motherfucker?
¿Qué mierda quieres, hijueputa?

What did you say to me?
¿Qué me dijiste?

Say that to my face, asshole!
¡Dímelo a la cara, pendejo!

Smack talk
Mentando madres

The blanket term for talking smack in Spanish includes lots of things more and less offensive than "mentioning one's mother by name"—but if you know someone's mother's first name, or worse, her maiden name, keep that one in your back pocket in case you need heavy artillery later on.

POPPYCOCK
PAVADAS

The suffix -ada(s), which can be tacked onto almost any noun in this chapter, often has a meaning like "shit Xs say/do," where X is any given category of person. Here are some common shenanigans that dipshits and fucknuts get up to, ranked generally from mild to spicy, although relative rankings like these vary regionally or by social circle.

Bolas → Bolada	White lie, con
Pavo → Pavadas	Frivolous things (turkey-talk); poppycock
Chocha → Chochada	Nonsense, trifling shit
Capullo → Capullada	A stupid thing to say
Gil → Giladas	Screw-ups, major faux pas
Huevos → Huevadas	Dumb shit
Chancho → Chanchadas	Nasty sexual shit, done or said (*chancho* = hog)
Verga → Vergada	A dick-up; dick-talk
Chucha → Chuchada	A swindle, a con
Puta → Putada	A nasty, dirty trick
Chingar → Chingada (Mex)	Fuck-all, shitshow
Peruano → Peruanada	A shitshow Peruvian-style (Curiously, Peruvians say this too!)
Pendejo → Pendejadas	Dipshiteries
Cagar → Cagadas	Fuck-ups

I can't stand that bitch!
¡No aguanto a esa puta!

She's such a gossip!
¡Qué chismosa!

He thinks he's the shit.
Él piensa que es la hostia. (Spn)

He's all bark and no bite.
Mucho ruido y pocas nueces.

What a freak!
¡Qué frik! | ¡Qué friki! (Spn)

She's such a Debbie Downer.
¡Qué rebajón!

An opportunist like her is always waiting to **stab you in the back.**
Una veleta como ella siempre está dispuesta a darte la puñalada trasera.
Una veleta means "weather vane," as in, someone that faces wherever the wind's blowing.

Did you see what she wore to the show last night?
¿Viste lo que tenía puesto anoche?

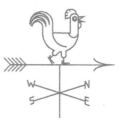

They're fake, definitely.
Seguro que son falsas.

I heard his dick is tiny.
Tengo oído que su verga es pequeñita.

OMG! Can you believe she actually showed up?
¡ALV (a la verga)! ¿Puedes creer que al fín vino?

Oh, **hell no**! He better not be talking shit about me!
¡Ni de coña! ¡Espero que no esté hablando pestes de mí! (Spn)

SCORES OF WHORES
PUTEANDO A LAS PUTAS

Spanish has so many words for actual sex workers that, over time, half of them have become relatively benign (if still misogynistic) terms that you might hear used not only for suspected sex workers, but also for slutty amateurs, or even for ex-girlfriends the speaker isn't even particularly mad at.

Bitch	*Puta*
Tramp	*Mujerzuela*
Skank	*Una macarra* (*un macarra* is a pimp!)
Floozy	*Golfa*
Slut	*Pelandusca* | *cuero* (Carib, Andes)
Ho	*Hortera; Gata* (S.Cone)
Hoochie	*Guarra* | *Yiro* (S.Cone)
Trick	*Furcia* | *Lumi* (Spn)
Whore	*Zorra* | *Jinetera* (Mex, Carib)

Hooker	*Fulana* (also means "random girl") | *Pendón* (Spn)
Prostitute	*Ramera* | *Guaricha* (Andes)

He is such a **deadbeat**.
*Él es un **haragán** total.*

Don't be stupid
No seas gil

The most basic and prolific Spanish insult is an attack on one's intelligence. It's a good place to start no matter what the subject matter, and you can lob a few wit-grenades this way without tripping too many alarms. Save the sexual stuff and the mom stuff for later, unless you're ready for that first swing already.

You're **kinda stupid**, aren't you?
*Eres **medio tontito/a**, ¿no?*

Were you born this **slow**, or did that just happen recently?
*¿Naciste **lento/a**, o pasó recién?*

The kid's got **rocks for brains**. He's **totally out to lunch**.
*Este chico tiene **piedras por sesos**. Es **totalmente lelo**.*

Don't be such a....
No seas....

That fat American is a flat-out....
Ese/a yanqui gordo/a es un/una....pleno.

> **dummy**
> *gil*
> You can dress this one up as *un flor de gil*, which translates to "a royal dumbass."

dumbass
gilún
When dumbasses travel in packs, you can refer to the herd as *una gilada*, or "a gaggle of dumbasses."

dumbfuck
gilazo | *gilipollas* (Spn)

bag of rocks
maleta

layabout, do-nothing
flojo (S.Am) | *batatero* (Carib)

doofus
buey | *güey* (Mex)
Literally, "ox."

blockhead
adoquín | *cuadrado/a* (S.Cone)

serious scatterbrain
pasmado/a

moron
mamerto/a | *panoli* (Spn)

nitwit/dimwit/halfwit
baboso/a; atarantado/a; tarado/a

numbskull
huevón

mentally deficient
infradotado/a | *oligofrénico/a* (S.Cone)

Talkin' 'bout yo' mama
Mentándote la madre

When you're ready to take the confrontation out of first gear, try out one of the following aspersions on someone's character or heritage. They're guaranteed to bring on a case of what Spanish speakers call *mala sangre.*

You're nothing but a....
No eres nada sino un/una....

What a....!
¡Qué....!

> **son of a bitch**
> *hijueputa; 'jueputa; joputas | juepuchas* (S.Cone)
>
> **creep**
> *desgraciado/a*
>
> **piece of trash**
> *basura*
>
> **motherfucker**
> *conchesumá* (S.Cone)
> From *concha de su madre* ("his mother's cunt").
>
> **royal asshole**
> *hijo de la gran po*
>
> **bastard**
> *guacho* (S.Cone)
>
> **prick**
> *carepicha* (CenAm)
> From *cara de picha* ("dick face").
>
> **cocksucker**
> *chupapollas*
> Yes, this term connotes as much homophobia in Spanish as in English.
>
> **fucker**
> *ojete*
>
> **fuck-up**
> *mamón*

abomination
aborto
Literally, "abortion."

born asshole
malparido
Literally, "badly born," or "miscarriage that survived."

vermin
insecto

worm
larva

Go to hell
Vete al carajo

The purest Spanish curses are two-part recommendations: First, they tell their recipients to get lost, then, they helpfully offer an activity for them to do once they're gone. That latter activity can range from benign stuff, like flying a kite, to more serious ill-will, like being killed, anally penetrated, and so on. Bonus points for creativity!

Clear out! Get lost! Scram!
¡Corta campo! ¡Aléjate! ¡Rájate!

Go fly a kite!
¡Vete a espulgar un galgo!
Literally, "Go deflea a greyhound."

Go to hell!
¡Vete a la porra!

Go wipe your ass!
¡Anda a limpiarte el culo!

Go fuck yourself!
¡Cáchate! (Per)

Fuck you!
¡Chíngate! (Mex) | *¡Que te den!* (Spn)

Fuck off!
¡Ándate bien al carajo!

Go get fucked!
¡Andate a joder! (S.Cone)

Don't set foot in here again or I'll put you in a cast lickety-split.
No vuelves a poner pie aquí o te lo pongo en un yeso rapidingo.

Go to hell and **put a finger in your ass** when you get there!
¡Vete al diablo y métete el dedo en el ojete cuando llegues!

Why don't you take that billy club and **go fuck yourself with it**?
¿Por qué no te llevas ese bolillo y te lo metes en el culo?

Go try your bullshit on the hooker that spawned you!
¡Ándate a cantar tus pavadas a la ramera que te parió!

Go to the rotten cunt of your whore mother!
¡Vete al coño podrido de tu puta madre!

Talkin' shit
Diciendo cagadas

Spanish speakers inherited the Roman obsession with poop, or specifically, the idea that a civilization should be judged by the sophistication of its plumbing. This is why the strongest cussword in Spanish is not "fuck" or "cunt," but "shit." And the most dramatic form of shitting (and the mother of all Spanish insults) is to shit on one's enemies, to wipe one's butt with their sacred things, and to otherwise tarnish someone with defecation.

I shit on...!
¡Me cago en...!

my totally bitch-ass ex-boyfriend/girlfriend
mi re-que-te-jodido/a ex-novio/a

The prefix *re-*, and the doubly emphatic *requete-*, amplifies other adjective in a cheeky, slangy way.

my asshole of a **boss**
*el huevón de mi **jefe***

crooked-ass Customs—let them fleece the next guy
la aduana chingona—que chinguen al próximo

the Host (of the Eucharist)
la hostia

This anti-Catholic expletive refers to the toiletbowl-like gesture made by the cupped hands of the priest administering the Eucharist.

the head of Benito Juárez
la cabeza de Benito Juárez

You might hear fervent Catholics uttering this one, as Benito Juárez is still detested in the God-fearing world for separating church and state.

my perverted **neighbor**
*mi **vecino** perverso*

the ridiculous toupee of Petey Wilson
el peluquín ridículo de Piti Wilson

Pete Wilson was formerly California's governor and chief supporter of Proposition 187, which stripped illegal immigrants of government services and basic human rights. Until the 45th president of the United States was elected, he was still cursed and remembered by Californian Latinos as an all-time villain.

my idiot of a president
el idiota de mi presidente

your mother's torn-up, whoring cunt
el coño reventado de tu madre ramera

This is the H-bomb of all Spanish curses.

Fightin' words
Palabras peladas

The best part of any barfight is the moment just before fists start flying, when the two parties are talking about all the nasty things they're going to do to each other and how hard they're gonna fuck each other up. As in many cultures, the line between violence and sex can be blurred disturbingly by otherwise very macho and homophobic speakers, with little regard for the gender performances of the people involved.

I'm gonna **kick your ass!**
*¡Te voy a **madrear!** (Mex)*

I'm gonna **tie** you **in knots.**
*Te voy a **atar en nudos.***

Take it easy, I don't wanna have to **knock you to pieces.**
*Tómalo con calma, no quiero tener que **reventarte.***

I'm gonna crack that hollow gourd of yours in half!
*¡**Te voy a partir** esa calabaza vacía!*

I'm gonna **open a can of whoop-ass** you won't soon forget!
*¡Te voy a **dar una paliza** de recuerdo!*

Keep givin' me the stinkeye, and I'm gonna **make mincemeat** out of you!
*¡Sigue con la ojeriza y te voy a **hacer polvo**!*

He's gonna **whoop** me **like an eggbeater!**
*¡Me va a **batir como la crema para la torta**!*

I'm gonna **mop the floor with your hideous face**, you scumbag!
*¡Te voy a **usar la cara espantosa como trapo de piso,** canalla!*

You're gonna get **ripped to shreds!**
*¡Te va a dejar **harapiento**!*

I'm gonna **fuck** you **up royally**!
*¡Te voy a **hacer una mierda líquida**!*
Literally, "I'm gonna make liquid shit out of you."

I'm gonna **go medieval on your ass**!
*¡Voy a **practicar el medioevo con tu culo**!*

Punches and kicks
Golpes y patadas

The great thing about Spanish is the precision afforded by its
suffixes, perhaps the coolest of which is *-azo*. When added to the
end of a noun, it basically means "the act of being smacked by
(that noun)." So if your girlfriend throws dishes at you and lands
one, it's *un platazo*; if you throw the cat right back at her, it's *un
gatazo*; if the wall crashes on her, it's *un paredazo*, and so on.

Did you see that **punch**?
*¿Viste ese **puñetazo**?*

He **smacked** him good.
*Le **zumbó** bien.* | *...**sonó**...* (Mex)

She **broke his nose** with that **bitch slap**.
*Le **rompió la nariz** con ese **cachetazo**.*

I'm gonna **haul off and deck you** if you don't shut your mouth.
*Te voy a **dar una paliza súbita** si no te callas la boca.*
La paliza súbita, "the sudden whoop-ass," can refer to a hurricane or just an
unexpected and devastating swat to the back of the head, particularly from a
parent.

I **backhanded** that fool and gave him a **black eye**.
*A ese gilazo le dí **un sopapo trasero** y le dejé con un **ojo morado**.*

Damn, you just **knocked him out** cold!
*¡Híjole, que **lo dejaste** frío!*

You **slap** like a girl.
*Das **guantazos** como una nena.*
Literally, "glove slaps," like for a duel.

I'm gonna **uppercut** your face.
*Te voy a **dar un ganchazo** en la cara.*

I'll **karate chop** you in the neck.
*Te voy a **dar un hachazo de karate** en el cuello.*

Kick him in the nuts!
*¡**Patéale** en los huevos!*

Put him in a **headlock**!
*¡Ponle en una **llave de cabeza**!*

Did you see that?! She picked him up and **put him in a pile driver**!
*¿Viste eso? ¡Lo agarró y **le hizo el martinete**!*

I'll **kill** you, asshole!
*¡Te voy a **carnear**, pendejo!*

Chill out
Cálmate

If you ever find yourself in a Latin American shantytown without a police squadron of protection, you may want to hide the shiny digital camera and start remembering some of these phrases.

Can't we all just **get along**?
*¿No podríamos **llevarnos bien** nomás?*

Quit it, boys, **break it up**.
*Basta, chicos, **déjenlo**.*

Take it outside.
Llévalo afuera.

Calm the fuck down!
¡Cálmense, carajo!

Dude, **get a hold of yourself!**
¡Contrólate, chavo!

Don't flip out!
!No flipes!

Slow down, tough guy.
Frénalo un poco, macho.

Get off it, man!
¡Déjelo, hombre!

Just **forget about it.**
Olvídalo nomás.

It's not worth it.
No vale la pena.

Let's all just take it easy.
Tomémoslo con calma.

I'm not **looking for a fight, and** I don't want any **trouble.**
*No estoy **buscando riña** y tampoco quiero **bulla** ninguna.*

Relax, I was **just playin'.**
*Calma, era un **chiste nomás.***

Make love, not war.
Haz el amor, no la guerra.

Who wants a **group hug**?
*¿Quién quiere un **abrazo en grupo**?*

CHAPTER 7

Pop Culture & Technology
Lo Popular & Lo Tecnológico

Americans sometimes have trouble shaking free of a stereotype in which everyone south of the border is a rustic farmhand sleeping against a cactus or piling sacks onto a *burro*, but urban Latin Americans are as tech-savvy and *actualizados* (up to date) as urban people in the developed world. In fact, when it comes to telecommunications, piracy, and privacy, the average Latin American person might be far more knowledgeable, since disposable income is tight and jobs are a lot easier to lose. Whether burning bootleg DVDs, finding community-written subtitles to anime ripped off TV, sending dirty text messages to a mistress, Skyping and WhatsApping with friends on other continents, or downloading cracked apps via torrent, the Spanish speaker of the twenty-first century tends to be pretty media-savvy.

The TV
La tele

Television shows in Spanish are essentially the same as those in English, with two notable exceptions: there's more nudity and more crying. Whether you're tuned to news coverage, nature documentaries, police dramas, soap operas, game shows, or even cable-access shows about UFOs, you're pretty much guaranteed a public display of emotion and/or cleavage every ten minutes.

Keep **channel surfing,** and I'm gonna shove **the remote** up your ass.
*Sigue **haciendo zapping** y voy a meterte **el remoto** en el ojete.*

What's on TV?
¿Qué hay en la tele?

Sábado Gigante

This kitschy hodgepodge of a game show, talk show, kids' show, and sketch comedy was filmed live for eight straight hours every Saturday for 24 years in Chile, and then in Miami for another 29. Even though its run is over, it is so legendary 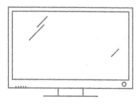 it still bears mention. Even after ending his stint as regular host when the show moved to Miami, it's been synonymous with its charismatic original host, "Don Francisco." All over Latin America and in the Latino U.S., Don Francisco is a household name whose show generally rates higher than any locally produced competition.

Showmatch

Argentina's top-rated variety show continually morphs genres to hold down its spot in the rankings, phasing in and out new formats (mini game shows, sketch comedy miniseries, and so on). In between new ideas, though, they stick to classics, like getting comedian Yayo (Adam Sandler meets Howard Stern) to offend starlets with dirty jokes, then following the ensuing confrontations and offstage hissy fits with a handheld camera, Jerry Springer–style. Also, there's plenty of nudity and crying, and celebrity smalltalk round tables. It's like crystallizing Argentine TV and mainlining it.

Los Conquistadores del Fin del Mundo

The survival reality subgenre has been huge in Latin America. The biggest of the bunch have been *Expedición Crusoe* (the same as our *Survivor*) and *Los Conquistadores del Fin del Mundo* (similar to *The Amazing Race*). Filmed in the Argentine Patagonia, contestants on *Conquistadores* race to the famous "End of the World Lighthouse" in Ushuaia. There's even an edition in which only pure-blooded Basques can compete!

Cantando/Bailando por un Sueño (Mexico and Argentina)

Like *Dancing with the Stars*, professional singers or dancers pair up with a celebrity of the opposite sex to sing or dance a duet. But since the Mexican version blew up the charts by substituting singing for dancing, Argentina had to up the ante and produce ice-skating with the stars. A musical-comedy version of *Cantando por...*is in the works, as well as a spin-off devoted to (I kid you not) competitive swimming. At press time, a partial list of guests on the 12th season of BPUS was announced by perennial Argentine talking head Marcelo Tinelli at a press conference that was (god help us all) front-page news in Buenos Aires.

Los Héroes del Norte

You might not expect a sitcom heavy on musical numbers about the misadventures of a country band to top ratings charts and rake in awards, but the writing, all-star cameos, and deeply Mexican sense of humor combined to ensure that this *Spinal Tap*–esque show has done both for half a decade and counting.

Kassandra

This Venezuelan soap powerhouse about a gypsy marrying into money is one of the most syndicated and re-run dramas ever. It also holds the Guinness record for most *exported* Spanish-language television show, with 128 countries having picked it up. During its bloody civil war, Serbia was one of these 128. Curiously, the daily cease-fire in Sarajevo coincided with the hour *Kassandra* aired. Coincidence?

Marimar

To Mexicans, *Marimar* was just another vendetta-filled *telenovela* about a working-class girl, her Prince Charming, and the backbiting bitches in the prince's family. But as often happens, it was a bigger hit internationally than at home for unknowable reasons of cultural difference. When it was broadcast during Ramadan of 1997, it caused such a sensation that a council of Muslim clerics in Abidjan, worried about the show's popularity, rescheduled evening prayers to keep up mosque attendance! In more recent times, the soap operas that dominate the Mexican and U.S. markets (*Eva, La Trailera, Tres Veces Ana, Pasión Y Poder*) have stuck to this centuries-old plot formula derived, perhaps, from the bestsellers of over a century ago.

El Cartel de los Sapos; Rosario Tijeras; El Señor de los Cielos; El Cartel, Nada Personal

The only thing more volatile, organically complex, and melodramatic than a Latin American extended family is an international drug cartel—and much to the chagrin of D.A.R.E.-types and scandalized viewers around the world, Mexico and Colombia's best-rated dramas, melodramas, action shows, and even comedies are increasingly focused on the drug industry, which is increasingly central in pop culture.

Los Hombres de Paco

This cop-drama about a somewhat incompetent trio of idiot cops is currently Spain's top-rated fiction show, even though it has heaping helpings of black comedy and social commentary, two things notoriously absent from American prime time.

The movies
Las pelis

Usually, the names of American movies are given direct Spanish translations when they're released abroad. But the monolingual lackeys who slave away in studio think tanks occasionally decide on titles that make those online translation websites look graceful: *101 Dalmations* nonsensically became "Night of the Cold Noses," *Mrs. Doubtfire* turned into the saccharine (and tone-deaf) "Your Dad Forever," and *Brokeback Mountain* was given a title that I'm pretty sure was stolen from a Hardy Boys novel: "The Secret in the Mountain."

Let's go see a...**on the big screen.**
Vámonos a ver un/una...en pantalla grande.

How long has that...**been running?**
¿Desde cuándo está en cartel ese/esa...?

> **tearjerker**
> *lacrimógena*
>
> **cartoon**
> *dibujo animado*

screwball comedy
comedia blanca

meathead movie
película machote

chick flick
peli melosa

feel-good hit of the year
éxito sensacional de optimismo ligero

documentary
documental

B movie
película "serie B"

porno
porno

Is it **dubbed**? Cuz it's just not the same without Sean Connery's Scottish accent.
*¿Está **doblada**? Porque no es la misma cosa sin el acento escocés de Sean Connery.*

Who cares if it has **subtitles**? I can't read that fast.
*¿A quién le importa si tenga **subtítulos**? Yo no leo tan rápido.*

Comics
Los cómics

Comics are *huge* in the Spanish-speaking world. People of all walks of life read cheap comics in a whole range of genres that we simply don't have in the United States. Granny flips through her B&W soap operas, Gramps mutters into his bound anthology of yesteryear's political cartoons, your nephew flips manically through corral shootouts in Wild West comics (yup, to this day!), the goth kid next to you chuckles into his true-crime slasher, and the hormone-case across the aisle isn't trying hard enough to hide the boner his cheesecake pinup comics are giving him. High-brow "art comics" are as big in Spain and Latin America as just about anywhere, except maybe France and the Pacific Northwest. Even the pamphlets that Jehovah's Witnesses put in your hand are surprisingly stylish bits of comic art!

In Latin America in particular, they're still a major art form and mass media entertainment. Here are some landmarks from the golden age of comics right up to the present.

Memín Pinguín
(Mexico: 1940s, 372 issues, continuously in print/reprint ever since)

Mafalda
(Argentina: 1964–1973) This international favorite about a precocious and bossy grade schooler was modeled on Charles Schulz' *Peanuts* in visual style and in its wholesome sense of humor, but its stronger political undertones got its author publicly exiled to Mexico.

Condorito
(Chile: 1955–1985) Less political and intellectual than *Mafalda* (and thus, continuously published for over 40 years)

Supercholo
(Perú: 1955–1966; 1994–1998)

Mortadelo & Filemón
(Spain: 1955–present)

Los Agachados
(Mexico: 1968–1981)

Revista Fierro
(Argentina: 1984–1992; 2006–present)

Where are your...?
¿Dónde tiene usted las...?

Are this week's...in?
¿Ya tienes las...de está semana?

> **comic strips (typically sold in anthologies)**
> *tiras cómicas*

political cartoons (single-frame political comics)
viñetas políticas

comic books
historietas; tebeos (Spn) | *moneros* (Mex)

soap opera comics
comics sentimentales

kids' comics
comics infantiles

Japanese comics
comics manga

Pop music
Música "pop"

In Latin America, Pop music and shantytown music have had a complicated and rich relationship bordering on symbiosis since long before gangster rap turned suburban malls worldwide into a carnival of white-kid posturing. These are the hotter currents in Spanish-speaking pop music nowadays, for better or for worse.

Let's listen to some....
Ponnos algo de....

Bump that....
Súbele a esa....

I can't stand....
No soporto....

Norteñas

Norteñas are border songs, ballads about *coyotes* (people-smugglers) and *narqueros* (drug-smugglers) set to an evolved *banda* (border-country) tune that's lighter on the polka backbeat than the previous generation's version of *banda*. You might think tubas and accordions would be uncool, but *Norteño* music has dominated the lion's share of Mexico's domestic market for decades, and shows no signs of loosening its grip now that young people living through drug-war hell have latched onto the *narco-norteño* subgenre (censorship scandals and distributor boycotts only make young people love it more, duh!)

Cumbia

This term refers to a whole family of pop genres including everything from saccharine sing-alongs to Timberlakey pop to dance-party jams, all featuring an Andean blend of catchy hooks; solid, danceable backbeats; and melodies even a blacked-out drunk could tap along to from the floor. The lyrics tend to be salt-of-the-earth, the instrumentation jangly and keyboardy, and the clubs where it's DJ'ed insipid and Budweiser-esque. But even at its worst, *cumbia* is like a good wedding band: functional for everyone, irritating to no one, the lowest common denominator from North to South.

Reggaetón

Around the time Shaggy and Sean Paul were bringing Jamaican "Dancehall" to the U.S., pop stars like Tego Calderón, Don Omar, and Calle 13 (think Jay-Z, 50 Cent, and Ludacris, respectively) started adapting the genre to the palates of Latin American listeners. The production is less smoked-out than its Jamaican cousin, with lyrics closer to top-40 hip-hop than gangsta rap, and the decades since have seen the genre grow sillier and poppier under the leadership of stars like Pitbull, but it is still essential to the Carribbean diaspora and isn't hard to find at dance clubs anywhere Spanish is spoken.

Perreo

This Puerto Rican predecessor to *Reggaetón* has all but disappeared into the dustbin of pop music history. However, the name ("doggy-business") is still used to refer to hardcore bumping and grinding, or *sexo vestido* ("sex with clothing on").

Soca

Across the smaller islands of the Carribbean, there is a common set of high-tempo beats that evolved out of Carneval's frenetic dance traditions and late '90s techno/dance hardware, often combining Island English, French Creole, and deeply accented Spanish in one song. In fact, it's something of a badge of pride for *soca* bands to have a song in each language, even if their singers can barely speak them, leading to some hilarious results.

But when you've been drinking for days and dancing at that breakneck speed, who can even hear the difference?

Salsa

Outside of a few specific places, *salsa* is as dorky and pony-tailed as it is in suburban America, no matter how short the skirts, how high the heels, or how slutty the after-parties. I'm only including this among real pop genres to discourage some persistent rumors to the contrary.

Funk Carioca (aka Baile funk)

What's not to love about hypnotically simple early hip-hop and late funk beats, and remarkably crude lyrics about car stereos and big asses? Younger readers more familiar with Crunk and Baltimore House might find it too hokey and cheerful, but *funk carioca* is really a revival of Miami Bass, where all that dirty south business started and where twerking was invented. The mythology around its *favela* origins aside, this sound has evolved into a standard at big-city dance clubs and electronic-music festivals alike.

Ibiza

Thanks to mammoth dance clubs like Manumission (capacity 10,000) and various electronic-music festivals, this resort island in Baleares, Spain has long rivaled Berlin as the epicenter of Europe's dance club culture. Its name, when used as an adjective, refers to boiled-down, slightly sleazy house music somewhere between vintage Detroit Techno and a car-commercial version of Acid House.

Don't laugh, but I'm secretly a huge fan of Juanes.
No te ries, pero soy un fan de Juanes.

I love Charly García! I even like his recent CDs.
Amo a Charly García! Hasta me gustan los nuevos discos.

What's your favorite band?
¿Cúal es tu banda favorita?

I heard El Guincho is **playing a gig** at a bar tonight.
*Tengo oído que El Guincho va a **tocar un bolo** en un bar a la noche.*

I really like the chorus of this song.
Me encanta el coro de está canción.

Computer-ese
Jerga informática

Like anywhere else in the world, most techie lingo is just barely transliterated English. But for the sake of teaching by example, here are the less obvious basic terms. If you really want to learn computer-ese, though, set the language to Spanish on your OS, your cell phone, and your software, and then teach yourself the hard way.

Does your apartment have **broadband**?
*¿Tu departamento tiene **banda ancha**?*
Cable dominates over DSL most everywhere, but both are usually called *banda ancha.*

There's a movie I've been trying to compress and **upload to you** on torrents.
*Hay una peli que vengo tratando de comprimir y **subirte** por torrent.*
Just as *subir* means "to upload," *bajar* means "to download."

My **desktop**'s totally fucked.
*Mi **compu de casa** está jodida.*

E-mail it to me as an **attachment** so I can **print it out**.
***Mándamelo** como **archivo adjunto** para que lo pueda **imprimir**.*

Where'd you get that DVD that plays **bootlegs** and **DivX movies**?
*¿Dónde conseguiste ese DVD que toca los **piratas** y los **DivX**?*
Thanks to tiny SRT subtitle files that are legal to up- and download, international video piracy is now as easy as ripping the subtitle track off an American DVD. This allows Spanish-subtitled DivX files to appear months before the official DVD releases, and makes it easy for anime freaks slaving over dictionaries to clumsily gloss everything the studios won't pay professionals to translate.

Do I need a **password** to access your USB **drive**?
*¿Necesito **contraseña** para acceder tu **llavero** USB?*

What's your **login**?
*¿Cúal es tu **nombre de usario**?*

Are you **online**?
*¿Estás **en linea**?*

Check out my **website**.
*Mira a mi **sitio web**.*

It really blows my mind the things rappers tweet about.
Me vuela la cabeza las cosas que twittean los rappers.

My **off-brand player** holds twice as many MP3s as your **iPod**!
*¡Mi **reproductor de cuarta** guarda dos veces los MP3s que tu **iPod**!*

They traced the security breach to some **sketchy apps** on his tablet.
Rastrearon la violación de seguridad a unos apps dudosas en su tableta.

That **background** is a little inappropriate, don't ya think?
*Ese **papel tapiz** es poco apropiado, ¿no te parece?*

Fifteen minutes of **Googling** and the damn **Wikipedia** don't qualify as "research."
*Quince minutos de **Googlear** y el pinche **Wiki** no cualifican como "investigación."*

The **link** you sent me took me to **a furry porn,** you degenerate!
*¡El **enlace** que me mandaste me llevó a **un porno furri**, degenerado!*

Social network overload
Enredado social

Spanish-speakers are intensely social, in terms of hours per day spent interacting—so they've taken a shine to all the virtual forms of smalltalk, spam, and narcissistic self-promotion that we call social media.

I posted a link **on your wall**.
*Puse un enlace **en tu muro**.*

Friend me on Facebook.
Agrégame en Facebook.

Unblock me!
¡Desbloquéame!

Your profile pic is hilarious!
¡Tu foto de perfil está rebuena!

Did you take that one with a **selfie stick**?
*¿Usaste un **palito selfie** para esa?*

What do you use for a **screen name**?
*¿Qué usas como **nick**?; ...**handle**?*

Isn't that a **dating website**?
*¿Ese no es un **sitio de citas**?*

That site needs moderation, I keep getting unsolicited **dickpics** from randoms.
*Ese sitio necesita moderación, sigo recibiendo **foto-pollas gratuitos** de cualquiera.*

That comment section is a swamp, every fifth comment is "**send nudes.**"
*Ese **Comentarios** [sic] es un pántano, cada quinto mensaje dice "**manda nudes.**"*

·······································

Chatlingo
Chat

Text messaging and free-messaging platforms like WhatsApp and Kik are *huge* in Spanish-speaking lands—largely because neither Spaniards nor Latin Americans can afford to talk on the phone much, given the ruthless price-fixing and gouging of their telecom markets. Unfortunately for non-native speakers, spry youngsters keep raising the bar on cryptic abbreviations and acronyms, which date back to flip-phone days but somehow survive in the era of predictive typing.

I love you always	tq 100pre	*(te quiero siempre)*
What	q	*(que)*
Where	dde	*(donde)*
How much	qto	*(cuanto)*
When	qdo	*(cuando)*
Here	ak	*(aquí)*
Because	xq	*(porque)*
I don't know	nc	*(no sé)*
No	–	*(no)*
Sort of/More or less	+-	*(más o menos)*
At least	x-	*(por lo menos)*
Whatever/same to me	md=	*(me da igual)*
Also	tb	*(también)*
Bye	xau	*(ciao)*
Hope you're well	ktbn	*(que estés bien)*
Don't worry/NBD	ntp	*(no te preocupes)*
Nothing/Forget it	nd	*(nada)*
Idiot	won	*(huevón)*
Shit	mela	*(mierda)*
Love ya much	tkm	*(te quiero mucho)*
Gotcha/pwned	tkg	*(te cagué)*
Suck it	xupalo	*(chúpalo)*
Your mother's pussy	ctm	*(coño de tu madre)*

T kiero + q tdo l mndo, toy :D
Te quiero más que todo el mundo, estoy contento.
I love you more than all the world, I'm so happy.

Md=, won
Me da igual, huevón
I give zero fucks, bruh.

Uds fue a s bar nue? Dde qda?
¿Ustedes fueron a ese bar nuevo? ¿Dónde queda?
Did you guys go to that new bar? Where is it?

Qdo m aqrd t qnto. ta nfrm tdv?
Cuando me acuerdo te cuento. ¿Estás enfermo todavía?
I'll tell you when I remember. Are you still sick?

Stoi bn pro tmpko mx mjr tqG
Estoy bien, pero tampoco mucho mejor. Te quiero, G.
I'm better, but not much better, either. Love, G.

Fashion
La moda

Although, or maybe because, half the world's sweatshops and *maquilladoras* are in Latin America, big-city Spanish speakers can be as shallow and ruthless about a look as any of those catty amateurs on *Project Runway*. Here are some basics for clawing and hissing.

The Twiggy look is totally **in vogue**—quit eating now!
*El estilo Twiggy está muy **en boga**—¡basta de comer, ya!*

That dress....
Ese vestido....

> **is so cute**
> *está divino*
>
> **is so trashy**
> *es callejero*
>
> **is so skanky**
> *es de hortera* (Spn)
>
> **is so last season**
> *está pasado de temporada*
>
> **is so unflattering**
> *es poco favorecedor*

Is that **vintage**?
*Eso es **vintage**?*

Wearing a sports jersey to a funeral is pretty **tacky**.
*Ir a un entierro de camiseta deportiva es bien **chabacano**.*

Her **hipster** vibe is so fake. Her tattoos aren't even real!
*Su aire de **modernilla** es tan falso. ¡Falsos aún los tatuajes!* (Spn) | *...**cheta**...* (S.Cone)

Take off that beret, you look like a **yuppie** in a midlife crisis.
*¡Quítate esa boina, pareces un **yuppie** en crisis de edad.*

Faux snakeskin is really **trendy** right now.
*La piel de serpiente falsa está bien **de moda** al momento.*

I pretend I'm not into all that **bling-bling**, but when I see platinum and ice like that....
*Disimulo cualquier interés en el **blinblineo**, pero cuando veo a platino y hielo así....*

I think the Louis Vuitton bag my boyfriend got me is **fake**!
*Me parece que la bolsa Louis Vuitton que me regaló mi novi es **falsa**! | ...**trucha**!* (S.Cone)

Youth cultures
Tribus urbanas

Los rockeros
Rock has a totally different meaning in every Hispanic culture. In Mexico, the boundaries between black metal, stoner metal, punk, industrial, and butt-rock are pretty permeable, making anyone who likes any of the above a *rockero*. In Argentina, by contrast, *rockeros* are specifically aficionados of homegrown, Spanish-language *rock nacional*, as opposed to *rollingos* (classic rockers who put the Rolling Stones, The Who, and/or the Ramones above all else), and neither zealous sect has much in common with the unwashed masses who listen to the more-recent mainstream English-language rock and pop imports hogging the airwaves.

Aggros

In Nu Metal–crazed Chile, *los aggros* issued an ultimatum to *los rockeros*: Jettison your attachment to all rock subgenres that came before Nu Metal, throw out your Rolling Stones records, and stop washing your hair, or else we won't let you into our World of Warcraft clans! Unfortunately, large numbers of the *huevones* took them up on it, and Chile has been even less cool for it ever since.

Los punkeros (aka ponkeros)

The robust tradition of anarchism in Spain trickled down to Latin America when Spanish anarchists fled there after the Spanish Civil War, turning anarchy into a real way of life rather than just a fashion statement, as it was in the U.S. (with few exceptions). Latin American punks are therefore a little more rebellious and off-grid than their Anglo counterparts, less likely to get a job, and more likely to end up making pipe bombs than just silk-screening edgy slogans onto patches in their parents' garages.

Los marquitos

Subcomandante Marcos, leader of the Zapatista movement, maintains semianonymity to this day. After those massive "we are all Marcos" rallies where flash-mobs would don the Zapatista ski-mask "uniform," would-be Marcoses became affectionately known as *Marquitos*. But this pet name is slowly becoming reserved for middle-class poseurs who sport Che Guevara shirts and mall-bought Mayan man-purses, and who burn through the billable hours of their private English tutors to translate Rage Against the Machine lyrics.

Los "darks" (aka moribundos, góticos)

Goths are different in the Hispanic world, mostly because black lace is more grandma than edgy, and fake blood is a bit mundane after all the civil wars and the weekly "blood-drinking" at Mass. Hispanic goths are more into serial killers, sadomasochism, politics, Satanism, metal, and banned horror films than Victorian kitsch, synthpop, burlesque, and séances. There are thriving, multi-generational goth scenes in every big city in Latin America, but Mexico City might well be the world capital of adult goths who dress up 365 and permanently modify their teeth, eyes, tongues, etc.

Los bakalas; Los bakaleros

Once slang for "fresh," as in "fresh as Bilbao *bacalao* (cod)," this term then came to refer nostalgically to the golden age of Spanish dance club culture. Nowadays, though, Spaniards use the word as a derogatory way to refer to MDMA burnouts and tacky 16-year-olds bumpin' goa-trance in their lowered Hondas.

Los emos; Los sensibles

Yup, same as at your high school—the sensitive kids wear sweaters and Converse All-Stars. They like sappy screamo and they slouch a lot. Their doting moms probably sewed those precious little homemade patches onto their Jansports for them. In 2008, there was even a wave of mobs bullying the emos at schools all across Mexico, some of whom organized on an anonymous reddit-style chat forum called "Anti-Emo Death Squad" that was full of homophobic rants about "emosexuals." However, the primping and Smiths sing-alongs show no signs of abating. If anything, the term (and the style) has chugged on as a stalwart subculture in working-class Mexico, although thankfully, the music they listen to has skewed away from screamo-rock and back to early goth standards and new bands like Mexrissey (an all-star Mexican Morrisey tribute band selling out stadiums in both Mexico and the U.S.).

Los niños bien | el chetaje (S.Cone) | los yeyés (Pan) | los pijos (Spn)

Yes, even the poorest corners of Spain and Latin America boast a robust leisure class, and each country has its own name for the well-heeled party animals. This group tends more toward the overtanned-Eurotrash, stone-washed-jeans look than the American country club preppy set, and their musical tastes tend toward Europe's big techno festivals and their local (incredibly expensive) counterparts.

Los poperos (aka poppis)

Want to sport a glossy subcultural persona without all the reading and social conflicts required to be being anti-anything? Why not join the rank and file of the pretty boys and baby dolls who can't think of anything better to identify with than asinine Shakira-style pop music! It's "hurrah for everything" every day for these perky little bottles of Prozac.

CHAPTER 8

Sports & Games
Deportes & Juegos

....

Soccer
Fútbol

Wherever Spanish is spoken, there is one sport that trumps all others in importance and viewership by a long shot—football. Not the kind with quarterbacks and piles of sweaty men pulling each other to the ground with nickel defenses and shotgun formations, but the *real* kind: *fútbol*. Many of the key terms used to talk about football are easy enough for an English speaker to pick up because, well, they're transliterated English words, including that monosyllabic word that sports announcers belt out for 90 seconds at a time. Lots of other UK slang (like *heel*, for instance) entered the Spanish lexicon through British soccer culture, announcers, coaches, and league exchanges.

Who's your favorite...?
¿Cuál es tu...favorito?

I wanna kill that...!
¡Quiero matar a ese...!

That...is legit.
*Es **chévere** ese...* (Mex, Carib) | *...**bárbaro**...* (S.Am) | *...**bestia**...*

That...sucks.
Es una mierda ese...

team
equipo

franchise
club

forward
delantero/a
This is the guy who scores all the goals, takes his shirt off, and goes running around the field with his arms out like an airplane.

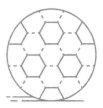

defender
defensa
This is one of the guys who plays in back and has thighs like tree trunks.

sweeper
líbero/a
This guy is the last line of defense between the defensive line and the goalie.

goalie
portero/a | golero/a (Mex)
If you don't know what a goalie is, you probably shouldn't even be reading this book.

coach
entrenador/a

referee
árbitro/a

How do I get to the **stadium/court**?
*¿Cómo llego a la **cancha**?*

Come on, let's see how cheap tickets are from that **scalper**.
*Vámonos, a ver como están de baratas las entradas de ese **revendedor/a**.*

Wanna grab a beer **at halftime**?
*¿Quieres conseguir una cerveza **entre medios**?*

Number 9 scored **a hell of a goal**.
*El nueve metió **un golazo**.*

KNOCK-DOWN, DRAG-OUT RIVALRIES
RIVALIDADES A BRAZO PARTIDO

You can't have a team without a rival team. And you can't have a rivalry without a major annual showdown that divides the country in half, cuts freeways, and requires lots of police overtime. Sports are all about the love, right?

Mexican League: Guadalajara vs. Club América

Guadalajarans think of Mexico City as full of wannabe Europeans. Residents of Mexico City consider Guadalajara to be the backward epicenter of country music, working-class culture, and all things rural and "old school." Guada's team, *los chivos*, almost never drafts a player born outside of Mexico. Club América's team, *las aguilas*, has a roster full of ringers poached from the international circuit and European leagues. Every match between these two teams re-stages the major political struggle of Mexican history, as evidenced in their nicknames: *los capitalinos y los provincianos*, or the Capital City kids and the Backwoodsmen.

Argentine League: Boca vs. River

These two Buenos Aires teams have been the major Argentine clubs for over a century. Boca, the name taken from the warehouse neighborhood at the mouth (*boca*) of the River Plata, are working-class heroes who've adopted the nickname *bosteros*, "manure shovelers." River, based among the English-speaking, country-club elites on the north (i.e., river) side of the city, is nicknamed *los millionarios*. The annual *superclásico* is such a spectator event that travel agencies sell package deals structured around it. But bring your riot gear! The mythology surrounding the teams sometimes turns the postgame riot into all-out class warfare that shuts down the city for days.

Spanish League: Barcelona vs. Real Madrid

The two biggest, most successful teams in Spain face off twice a year, pitting the two major cities of the country and the two poles of Spanish life against each other: Castilian civility vs. Cataluñian anarchy, standardized Spanish vs. Catalán, and mainstream politics vs. separatist solidarity. Team Barcelona, nicknamed Barça, is called the *culers* or *culés*, because their popularity outgrew their tiny stadium in the '20s and anyone walking by saw the *culos* of the last fans to arrive hanging over the stadium wall. Team Madrid, made up of pretty boys in white uniforms, gets called *los merengues* and sports a prominent royal crown on its team crest—which might handicap its popularity, if only they weren't so amazingly good (they hold the record for most European Cup titles).

What's the **score**?
¿Y el tanteo?

Their team **scored** two goals.
Su equipo marcó dos goles.

Gooooooooaaaaaaaaalllllllllllllllllllllllllllllllllllllllll!
¡Gooooooooooooooooooooolllllllllllllllllllllllllllll!

The *goooooooooooooool*-yelling tradition, which seems so timeless, was actually limited to Argentine radio and TV until the 1990 World Cup, when an Argentine (and Boca-loyal) sportscaster, Andrés Cantor, set the standard by which all future sportscasters would be measured. Like opera singing, it's all in the diaphragm muscle and circular breathing.

....

For the fans
Para los hinchas

Who do you **root for**?
¿A quién apoyas? | *¿Por quién hinchas?* (S.Cone)

I'm a fan of Boca.
Soy hincha de Boca.

Hincha is a term used only for soccer fans. For all other sports, fans are either *fanáticos* or *aficionados*.

I'm a **fan** of Real Madrid.
Soy un forofo de Real Madrid. (Spn)

You're one of those **hardcore, crazy fans**, aren't you?
Tú eres uno de esos ultras, ¿no?
Ultra as in *ultrafanático*, the chest-painting kind.

I'm not a **hooligan** or anything like that.
No, gamberro no soy, ni nada al estilo.
This refers to the violent, rioting type of fan.

That blind fuckin' **ref** doesn't see anything!
¡Ese silbante ciego de mierda no ve nada!
Literally, "whistle-blower."

Oh, come on, he shouldn't have called that!
¡Pero por favor, no debe haberlo pitado!
Careful: *Pitar* literally means "to blow a whistle," so it only refers to whistle calls.

Did the referee really just give him a yellow card for that?
¿En serio, el árbitro le dió una tarjeta amarilla por eso?

I'd have given him a red for it.
Yo le hubiera dado una roja.

Foul! Why doesn't he foul him?
¡Falta! ¿Por qué no lo falta?

It looks like he took a good foul just to thwart the forward's rush.
Parece que fue una falta táctica para detener el avance del delantero.

THE MANY FORMS THAT SUPPORT TAKES
LAS FORMAS QUE TOMA LA PORRA

All across Latin America, people live their fanaticism for their team in various, overlapping ways— many of which can be, confusingly, referred to by the same word, *porra*, in different contexts. Even more confusingly, the term can also mean "dumb" or "thickheaded," in addition to the "billy club" usage mentioned a few chapters ago. Don't get it twisted!

The **cheerleaders** for that team are beautiful.
Es hermosa la porra de ese equipo.

My sister wanted **to cheerlead** for them but they turned her away.
Mi hermana quería porrear por ellos, pero la rechazaron.

The brawls between **diehards** are serious every year when they play.
El choque de las porras es grave todos los años cuando juegan.

My friends and I set up **a betting pool** for the championship, are you interested?
Mis compas armamos una porra para el campeonato, te interesa?

The coach for that franchise is kind of a **bonehead**, and his nose got broken by a **billy club**.
El técnico de ese club es medio porro, con esa nariz rota por una porra.

I can barely hear you, everyone's **cheering so loud**!
*¡Apenas te oigo, todos están **alentando tan fuerte**!*

Look at the other team's **supporters**! They're gonna cry any minute!
*¡Mira **la barra** del otro club! ¡Se van echar a llorar!*

We are **the champions**!
*¡Somos **los/las campeones/as**!*

....

He's on fire!"
"*¡Está que le sale!*"

Half the fun of sports is the whole panoply of specialized cursing and poetic imagery that goes with it, which is how sportscasters are still a thing now that we have all the technology to see and hear what's going on for ourselves. Here are some basics to help get you started on the long road to decoding the banter of play-by-play announcers and SportsCenter repeats.

They're really **showing some hustle**!
*¡Se están **poniendo las pilas**!*
Literally, "putting in their batteries."

He's on a helluva **streak**!
*¡Está en una buena **racha**!*

Get your fat ass in gear!
¡Muévete las nalgas anchas!

Get across the field, already!
*¡Dale, **corta campo**!*

That referee is **blind as a bat**!
*¡Ese árbitro es un **murciélago**!*

Their defense is **pudding**.
*Su defensa es **un flan**.*

That defender's a real **pushover**.
*Ese defensa es un **queso** total.*

SOCCER PLAY TERMS
TERMINOLOGÍA FUTBOLÍSTICA

Clear the ball!
¡Patee por adelante!
It's also common in everyday speech to use this phrase as a metaphor for short-term crisis management, like the American "putting out fires."

Offsides
Fuera de juego

Header
Una cabecita

To dribble
Gambatear; Regatear

Quick pass
Lanzar | Chutar (Mex)
From the English, "Shoot!"

Passback, one-two
[Hacer una] pared

Delayed pass
Un pase retrasado; Una retrasada

Chip pass
Una vaselina corta

Lob
Una vaselina larga

Banana shot
Una vaselina curva
If you don't know what this means, look it up on YouTube.

Breakaway
Una internada

Bicycle kick
Una chilena

Nutmeg (to pass through the legs of the guy covering you)
Un túnel; Un caño (S.Cone) | *Una cacha* (Spn) | *Un huevo* (Par)

Hop (as in, pop over the head of the guy covering you)
Jopear (S.Cone)

That forward **is stiff as a cast**.
*Ese delantero **es de yeso***.

Check out **leadfoot** over there.
*Mira al **patadura** ese.*

He's total **deadweight**.
*Él es un **muerto** total.*

What an **oaf**!
*¡Qué **zafio/a**! | ...**croto**!* (S.Cone)

Stop being such a **crybaby**!
*¡Basta de hacerte el/la **llorón/as**!*

You call that offense, you **pussyfooting dandy**?
*¿Así juegas ofensa, **pechofrío remilgado**?*

They totally **demolished** us.
*Nos **dieron masa**.*

This actually means "they fucked us"—sports are as homoerotic in Spanish as in any language.

Did you see that **lob**? How the hell did he make **the nationals**?
*¿Viste a esa **masita**? ¿Cómo carajo llegó **a la [liga] nacional**?*

They're really **putting up a fight**!
*¡Mira si están **dándoles lucha**!*

It's gonna be **a fight to the bloody end**, fellas!
*¡Será **una lucha sin cuartel**, muchachos!*

For the players
Para los jugadores

Like in any other language, the set of words you need to yell at a television screen or all over the neck of the guy in the bleachers in front you is totally different from the set of words and phrases you'll need to play a pickup game in the park without getting benched.

We don't need to form a league or anything, let's just **kick the ball around**.
*No necesitamos formar liga y todo, juguémonos un **partidillo** nomás. | ... un **picadito**... (S.Cone)*

Where can I play a **pickup game** around here?
*¿Dónde podría jugarme una **pachanga** por aquí? | ...una **caimanera**... (Ven)*
Without the clarifying verb, people might think you mean the other use of the term *pachanga*: a swingin' party!

Pass it, he's **open**!
*¡Pásalo a él, que está **abierto**!*

Cover him, already!
*¡**Cúbrelo**, ya que ya!*

Pass it here! I'm **wide open**!
*¡Pásalo por aquí! ¡Estoy **solo**!*

Second-rate sports
Deportes de segunda

In most Spanish-speaking lands, anything but *fútbol* isn't really on the level of a "major sport." And if Spain weren't part of Europe, tennis and fencing and all those other fancy-boy sports would be as rare a hobby as in Latin America. The only real exception is the growing devotion to *Beisbol* in the Carribbean countries (and nowadays much of Central America as well), and old-timey sports "traditional" to a given area, but those are the only second-place sports that don't even come close to *fútbol*.

I play....
Yo practico al/a la....

I do....
Yo hago el/la....

Wanna go play some...?
¿Quieres ir a jugar...?

Is there any...on TV?
¿Hay...en la tele?

> **boxing**
> *boxeo*
>
> **basketball**
> *baloncesto*
>
> **tennis**
> *tenis*
>
> **swimming**
> *natación*
>
> **surfing**
> *el surf; el surfo; surfear*

Like most borrowed words, there isn't really a stable, accepted form for "surfing." Young people are more likely to use the more "Spanicized" forms, and in more formal contexts, people leave the English word in its original.

> **gymnastics**
> *gimnasia*
>
> **skiing**
> *esquí*
>
> **snowboarding**
> *snowboard*
>
> **karate**
> *karate*
>
> **ultimate fighting**
> *lucha hardcore*

Other sports
Otros deportes

Polo

Polo still looms large at the country-club end of the sports spectrum in Latin America. Since the Latin- and Anglo-American championships merged in 1987, Argentina and Brazil have won all but one title, with Chile and Mexico helping to keep America, England, and Australia out of the top three (except for one blip in 1995).

Kayak-polo

Yes, it is what it sounds like, and Spain has two televised competitive leagues of it. Go fig!

Pok-ta-pok

This Olmecan sport makes rugby look like a tea party. Each team has to somehow get a heavy, hemorrhage-inducing leather ball across an H-shaped court and through a hoop it barely fits in without using their hands or feet (tip: it's all in the elbows). The sport is played by Mayan-speaking communities throughout Southern Mexico and Guatemala, as well as in their recently growing diaspora in the U.S.

Lacrosse

Argentina and Spain both hold national championships and regularly send teams to the world championships. Although they may not be able to hold their own against the American, Canadian, and Iroquois teams when they get there, they are heroes back home for even qualifying.

Rugby

Another tooth-loosener that Argies and Spaniards really get behind is rugby, that sport with all the man-hugging, dog-piling, and fabulous stripey shirts.

Béisbol

It's no coincidence that some of the best Major League Baseball players come from the Caribbean. Baseball is huge in the Spanish-speaking Carribean and Central America south of Guatemala. The sport is big there, but it's a chicken-and-egg debate as to which came first: popularity, or exporting players.

Lucha Libre

Mexico's *luchas libres* are just as fake and theatrical as any WWF event, but the Mexican theatrical flair really comes out in the populist speeches the fighters deliver...*and* the vicious grandmothers in the audience screaming for blood.

VIDEO GAMES
VIDEOJUEGOS

Although kids in Latin America are crazy about video games, the process of getting adults to buy and play Wiis and Xboxes has been much harder to get going. The resistance to video games as "kid's stuff" is so deeply entrenched that many grown men with shrines to soccer heroes in their garages would slap me for even including this section in a chapter on sports.

Do you like playing video games?
¿Te gusta jugar videojuegos?

Know any good cheat codes for this game?
¿Conóces a algún código truco para este juego? (S.Am)

I've been stuck on this level for 21 hours.
Hace 21 horas que estoy en este nivel.

You just got totally owned.
Te acaban de ownear del todo.

He's not a novice, he's a total newb.
No es un novato, es un nuevón total.

Other activities
Otras actividades

I'm way into....
Estoy muy metido en lo de....

> **yoga**
> *el yoga*
>
> **backpacking**
> *el "trekking"*
>
> **hiking**
> *el senderismo*
>
> **darts**
> *los dardos*

foosball/table football
el futbolín/el metegol

pool
el billar

ping-pong
el ping pong

road biking
el bicicletismo

jogging
el "footing"

dominoes
el dominó

Dominó is more popular in the Caribbean than in just about any other part of the world; it's pretty easy to find a pickup game anywhere there. Just be careful they don't get the shirt off your back—it's a betting game, there more than here. Also note that in almost every Caribbean country, the rules are a little different.

bowling
bolos; bowling

Bolos can refer to American bowling or English bowls (aka *petanque*, bocce ball, etc.). For this reason, people increasingly use the English word to be more specific. *Un boliche* is the word for bowling alley in Mexico, but be careful when asking for directions to the nearest bowling alley in South America, where a *boliche* is a bar and a *bolín* ("bowling" pronounced quickly) is a brothel.

betting/gambling
la timba

....

Working out
Haciendo ejercicios

Not into the whole team-sports thing? Prefer sweating in a room full of mirrors with tacky pop music blaring and perverts pretending not to stare at you? Lucky for you, gym culture has caught on everywhere thanks to the viral monoculture of late capitalism. Nowadays, you can even find gyms in places that barely have running water!

Where is/are...?
¿Dónde queda/quedan...?

> **the treadmill**
> *las trotadoras; la caminadoras* (Mex) | *las cintas de correr* (Spn)

> **the stair machine**
> *la escaladora*

> **the exercise bike**
> *la bicicleta estacionaria*

> **the free weights**
> *los pesos libres*

> **the bench press**
> *la banca*

> **the pool**
> *la piscina; la pileta* (S.Cone) | *la alberca* (Mex)

I just did 1000....
Acabo de hacer mil....

> **push-ups**
> *las flexiones* | *las lagartijas* (Mex)
> *Lagartijas* literally means "lizards," which makes sense, since lizards are always kinda bobbing up and down on their arms.

> **pull-ups**
> *las dominadas*

> **sit-ups**
> *los abdominales; las sentadillas*

You're looking **ripped**!
*¡Te ves **macizo/a**!*

He must **work out**.
*Debe **entrenarse**.*

First, I'm gonna **stretch**.
*Primero, voy a **desperezarme.**; ...**estirarme.***

Wanna **go for a jog**?
*¿Quieres **salir a correr**? | ...**a trotar**?* (Mex)

I'm **out of breath, sore, and need a cigarette** desperately.
*Estoy **sin aliento, adolorido, y necesito un cigarrillo** desesperadamente.*

CHAPTER 9

Food & Drink
Comida & Bebida

Most Spanish speakers aren't pretentious or finicky about their food. Our culinary traditions skew toward the filling, efficient, and communal. We like honest fare cooked home-style, just the way *Mamá* made it. Related to this penchant for "honest" food is that we like to see our food being made. Open kitchens are anything but a flashy high-end gimmick, and precooked food is considered an abomination in most places.

Hunger
Hambre

I'm starving.
Estoy hambriento/a.

I'm so hungry that I'm dying.
Tengo un diente *que me estoy muriendo.*
In English, having a sweet tooth is a permanent condition; in Spanish, "having a tooth" is circumstantial.

I'm absolutely emaciated.
*Estoy **famélico**, pero mal.*

Let's get some....
Vamos a conseguirnos algo de....

> **food**
> *comida*

eats
manduca

junk food
comida basura | *comida chatarra* (LatAm)

fast food
comida rápida | *minutas* (S.Cone)

street food
garnacha (Mex)

ethnic food
comida étnica

Let's grab a quick bite to eat.
¿Comemos algo rápido por ahí?

I just want a snack.
Sólo quiero un bocadito | *...un piscolabis.* (Spn)

I want to stuff my face.
Quiero ponerme morado. (Spn)

Damn, you just inhaled those sopes!
¡Carajo, acabas de inhalar esos sopes!

I'm craving a little....
Me antoja un poco de....

> **barbecue**
> *barbacoa* (Mex) | *asado* (S.Cone)
> Did you know we get the English word "barbecue" from the Spanish, which gets it from the Arawakan language indigenous to Haiti and the Dominican Republic? They didn't have iron, but they still managed to get their meat slow-roasted on a *barbakoa*, or "framework of sticks."

> **Italian food**
> *comida italiana*
> Luckily for you, Italians immigrated en masse to Latin America during the same period they were flooding America's East Coast cities, setting up those amazing delicatessens in some nook or cranny of every sizable Latin American city. Pizza may get kind

of dodgy outside of the Southern Cone and Brazil, but in any Spanish-speaking city, a good mortadella sandwich or a plate of olivey pasta isn't hard to find.

chop suey/stir-fry

chaufa

The number of Cantonese immigrants to Latin America in the last century is second only perhaps to Italian and Spanish ones. There are "Chinese" restaurants in every Latin American city, but nowhere more so than in Perú, where the term *chaufa*, transliterated from the Cantonese *chowfun* (or *zhaofen* in Pinyin-Mandarin), retains both its literal meaning (fried rice) and its more general usage (greasy, no-frills takeout).

all-you-can-eat tacos

taquiza libre

In modern Mexico, tacos aren't restaurant food; they're practical, informal food that you can get at bars, on the street, in the parking lot of a sporting event, or at a market stall built from two milk crates. The term *taquiza* refers to "taco service"—as in, you contract the cart to serve your guests at a party, and they bring a portable kitchen and crank them out like a mobile factory. Meat-loving Mexicans respond to the words *taquiza libre* the way alcoholics respond to "open bar."

boneless, shell-less paella

paella ciega

In Spain and want the signature complex rice dish but can't be bothered to pick rabbit bones and clam shells out of your lunch? Just order it *ciega*. Ostensibly, they made it that way for blind people, but nowadays, lazy people are reaping the benefits. If you're at a real fancy place, you can even tell them how to cook it: soupy (*caldoso*), al dente (*meloso*), or crunchy (*soccorat* or *socorrado*).

suckling pig

lechón

An entire suckling pig may seem like an odd choice for loading up on a cart and selling in the street, but since they are very dense and retain heat, they can

still warm up the shivering masses hours after coming out of the oven, one little Dixie cup at a time. If you're the type who can't eat an animal after looking in its face, you might just want to keep walking and try and warm up with a hot beverage instead—it's traditional to display the apple-stuffed face prominently on the cart, sometimes still attached to the body and staring at you through steamy glass.

I'm full.
Estoy lleno/a.

I'm stuffed.
Estoy repleto/a.

I'm gonna burst!
¡Estoy quebrado/a!

Yum-yum!
¡Ñam-ñam!

It's really good!
¡Está buenísimo!

That was....
Eso era....

> **a good meal**
> *una buena comida*
>
> **really tasty**
> *muy sabroso*
>
> **delicious**
> *delicioso*
>
> **scrumptious**
> *riquísimo*
>
> **filling**
> *saciante*

Yuck!
¡Qué asco!

That's **foul.**
¡Eso es un asco!

Their food is crap.
Su comida es una mierda.

It's disgusting.
Es un asquete.

I think I just **lost my appetite.**
*Acabo de **perder el apetito.***

I think you just **cost me my appetite.**
*Acabas de **quitarme el apetito.***

A farmhand **wouldn't eat that shit** in the middle of a famine!
*¡Un peón **no comería esa mierda** en plena sequía!*

I'm not gonna eat....
No voy a comer....

> **this bullshit**
> *esta bosta*
> Literally, "manure."

> **this revolting garbage**
> *esta basura inmunda*

> **that abomination**
> *esa abominación*

> **this steaming turd**
> *esta cagada humeante*

Uhh...my stomach's really upset.
Uuu...me siento descompuesto.

I think those shrimp **gave me indigestion.**
*Me parece que esos camarones **se me indigestaron.***

Drinks
Bebidas

I'm thirsty.
Tengo sed.

My throat is parched. Could you give me...?
Tengo la garganta seca. ¿Me darías...?

some tap water
agua de canilla

IN VINO VERITAS
EN EL VINO ESTÁ LA VERDAD

Although both Spain and Latin America are huge and rapidly growing markets for beer, dominated by industrial pilsners, both also have centuries-old regional wine traditions, often markedly local in the varietals grown and the processes used. Here are a few regional variations you might want to try.

Txakoli
A Basque name for a green wine (*vinho verde* in Portuguese and Galician), this is a lightly effervescent early harvest white wine best served very chilled.

Tempranillo
A general term for early harvest wines from Spain, mostly applied to reds.

Garnacha
The Spanish name for *genache* grapes, and the blends it dominates.

Malbec
A high-altitude, hearty red traditionally paired with red meats and grown in the foothills of the Argentine and Chilean Andes.

Torrontés
A very lightly effervescent white wine from the arid foothills of the Northern Andes, which sometimes resembles Riesling.

Carménère
This ancient varietal, once the pride of Bourdeaux, was almost wiped out in France by a parasite and now accounts for a big chunk of Chile's high-end exports, since it grows well almost nowhere else on earth.

a sparkling water, no ice
un agua con gas, natural

very cold soda
una soda bien fría

a stupid-cold Coke
una coca casi congelada

a chocolate bar
una barra de chocolate

a hot chocolate
un chocolate
In Spanish, solid chocolate is the exception, not the norm—but in case you need to specify, a hot cocoa is a *chocolate en taza.*

a frappé
un granizado

a smoothie
un batido

a milkshake
un licuado; un batido de leche/crema

Get your juice on
Sacarle el jugo

Latin Americans love fruit juice almost as much as they love rich, meaty food—if not for fruit juice, they would be sitting ducks for the foreign laxative-industrial complex. In fact, in much of the Spanish-speaking world, the easiest place to find fresh, nutritious fruit juice is at fast-food places that specialize in meat-heavy sandwiches and takeout, which can be a real bummer for hungry vegans grossed out by the smell of a meat-covered griddle. The fruit is really next-level, though, and almost universally fresh and exactly ripe. Here are some exotic potables to try in your travels:

COFFEE TOURISM
TURISMO CAFEINADO

Juan Valdéz jokes aside (and please, let's keep them aside; growing up a Juan in America, you hear them all), coffee really is essential to the lifestyle and economy of much of the Spanish-speaking world. Nowadays, the trend in America is toward $5 artisanal masterpieces, but for a hundred years, most Latin Americans have paid well under $1 a cup for their morning fix and afternoon pick-me-up, allowing marathon workdays and all-night parties unheard of in the business-minded North. Maybe that's why the *siesta* is rapidly going extinct.

In the Caribbean, coffee is made in 2- to 8-shot stovetop aluminum espresso kettles called *cafetines*, a market cornered in the States by Italian exporter Bialetti. In South America, hourglass-shaped drippers called *milettas* make pragmatic coffee in extended-family pots, while urban elites sip individual shots of espresso (*café cortos*), micro lattes (*cortados*), and French-style mega lattes (*café con leche*) made in Italian machines. In Spain, as well as most of Latin America except Colombia and coffee-producing regions of Perú, it can still be hard to find coffee that hasn't been *torrado*, or roasted in oil sweetened with raw sugarcane that caramelizes onto the bean, creating a sugary-smoky overtone that some people find delicious and others worry might be cancerous. Mexicans have their own country-style variation on this cane-roasting process, which includes a heaping helping of astringent cloves thrown into the roasting pot (*olla*). Many grandmothers and old-fashioned restaurants offer this to their guests under the name *café de olla*: it's usually drip-filtered on the weak side, and adding milk is strictly taboo.

In most Latin American countries you can order an espresso "long" or "short" (*largo* or *corto*), but in Spain a single shot is a *café solo*, and a double is a *café doble*. In Spain, asking for a *café con hielo* will get you a small cup packed tightly with ice and an espresso shot for you to splash on at the last minute. In Latin America, presweetened iced coffee, American-style, is much easier to find in the warmer months, unless you're at the café of a museum or an opera house.

Every coffee lover should go to Colombia at least once in their life: Starbucks-style mega-chains compete nationwide for the urban takeout market, with new flavored syrups and slushy machines that you'd only see at a 7-Eleven in the U.S. Meanwhile, tiny boutiques vie for the high-end crowd, serving espressos lovingly pulled by hand while explaining to you the names of every hill and valley where each bean was hand-picked by an organic farmer they know called Luís. A national cooperative of Colombia's artisanal producers and roasters banded together to create a high-end brand that quickly slayed all these boutiques and smaller coops, opening branches not only across Latin America, but even in Miami and New York City (at time of press, you can stock up at nine American airports, plus those of Kuwait, Bahrain, and Malaysia!). By what name can this glorious coffee powerhouse by sought, you ask? In a curious act of *reconquista*, the nationalist cooperative actually bought back the name popularized by American conglomerate Yuban in the 80s— and Juan Valdéz Coffee was born.

Jugo de caña/Guarapo

Sugarcane is the basis for all kinds of drinks, most famously rum, its more primitive form *cachaça*, and its stronger distillation, *aguardiente de caña* (known to its friends as *caña, ron blanco, aguardiente de guarapo*, "why your grandpa doesn't see so well" or "where your college fund went"). But did you know that you can actually drink straight sugarcane juice if it's fresh enough, and that it's not nearly as sweet as you'd expect? When you're in a city in a sugar-producing country, listen for the sound of repurposed lawn mower engines and follow them to street vendors pulling sugarcanes out of giant bundles to fill tiny Dixie cups for a coin or two. Best with a touch of lemon, and counter-intuitively, good for the common cold.

Aguapanela

Another tooth-rotting beverage is Colombia's *aguapanela*, which is made by dissolving a brick of sugarcane (called a *panela, piloncillo* [Mex], *chancaca* [Per], *panocha*, etc.) in boiling water with a little lemon juice. Not your cup of tea? Then maybe you should go to the other end of the spectrum, like...

Zumo de amargo

In Seville, they grow some of the best citrus in the world—and also some of the most bitter, like the *naranjo amargo*. Even with substantial sugar added, this orange is so bitter that few places outside of Seville consume it in any form, aside from in Italian digestive bitters and tropical pork marinades. Bottoms up!

Jugo de cajú (pronounced kah-JOO) | *Jugo de merey* (Ven) | *Jugo de cajuil* (DoR) | *Jugo de marañon* (Carib)

Native to Brazil but cultivated in Venezuela and other Caribbean countries, the cashew nut is actually tiny in comparison to the fruit it grows attached to, but 94 percent of the cashew fruits grown commercially are thrown away after removing the prized nut. The other 6 percent are mostly used to make vinegar or to make an incredibly tart juice that takes a good bit of sugar to be palatable. Luckily, sugar usually grows cheaply nearby.

Vampiro

This classic Mexico City fruit blend is far removed from the palate most people stereotypically associate with Mexican cuisine. The name comes from the blood-red color imparted by raw beets, and celery brings a strong savory overtone that usually overpowers even the orange and pineapple juices. It is, however, the breakfast of choice for most *chilangos* (Distrito Federal natives)—it's just the thing to get you back to work after a heavy, spicy dinner and a tequila nightcap.

At the restaurant
En el restaurante

Service in the Spanish-speaking world isn't *bad*, exactly. It's indifferent to the point of performative cruelty. That's because there's little incentive, since tipping standards in most of Latin America range from zero, to the small coins left over after you pocket any bills in your change, to a whopping 10 percent in the biggest cities. It's not even that rude to leave no tip if you're short that week. But tip or no tip, the waitstaff won't "wait" on you: They do their own thing until you call, and if they don't like how you call them over, they play deaf, look busy, or pick up the phone to call their girlfriend. Much to the chagrin of the spoiled North American, this is one aspect of culture that Late Capitalism has yet to standardize, and is unlikely to any time soon.

Bring me....
Traígame....

> **the menu (more formal)**
> *la carta*

> **the menu (less formal)**
> *el menú*
> In much of South America, the lunch or dinner special is also called *el menú*.

> **the check**
> *la cuenta*

> **a bread basket**
> *una canasta de pan*

> **some steamed tortillas**
> *algunas tortillas al vapor*

> **the silverware**
> *los cubiertos*

Can we **order**?
*¿Podemos **pedir**?*

What would you recommend to a first-timer?
*¿**Qué recomendarías** a un principiante?*

Tell me, does *cuy* mean **guinea pig**?
*Dime, ¿cuy quiere decir **conejo de indias**?*

Five bucks if you can **name every organ** in my bowl of menudo.
*Cincuenta pesos si me puedes **nombrar cada órgano** en mi plato de menudo.*

What's taking so long? **Did they head out to the farm** to find my chicken, or what?
*¿Qué demora tanto? ¿**Se fueron al rancho** para elegir la gallina, o qué?*

THERE'S A WORM IN MY TEQUILA. CALL...
HAY UN GUSANO EN MI TEQUILA. LLÁMAME...

the manager
el gerente

your boss
tu jefe

the chef
el chef
If they actually pronounce it in proper French, you're probably paying too much for your food.

the cook
el cocinero

the waiter/waitress
el camarero/a

the dimwit that took my order
el/la lelo/a que me tomó el orden

the wine steward
el/la sommelier
It's French, and he probably is, too; you're not at a place serving local specialties.

the barbecue master
el/la asador/a
This is a proud profession and a guarded position in Latin America. The BBQ master ranks even higher than the chef in most kitchens.

Should we leave a **tip**?
*¿Debemos dejar una **propina**?*

I don't have any dough on me, but I could **do the dishes** to settle up.
*No tengo nada de billullo conmigo, pero podría **lavar los platos** para ajustar la cuenta.*

Mystery meats
Carnes ocultas

Much to the chagrin of Texas, "barbecue" isn't even an English word. *Barbacoa* was an old Latin American custom brought across the Rio Grande by Mexican cowherds, who, along with their counterparts in Spain and South America, had been getting their grill on for centuries. And after all that time heating their meat, they've come up with some pretty, um, "interesting" things to grill. I raise my fork to you, daring *asadores*!

Grill me up some...
Échame un poco de...en la parrilla.

How much protein is there in...?
¿Cuánta proteína hay en el...?

I'm on a strict diet of...
Estoy a dieta estricta de...

Chicharrón
Deep-fried strips of pork skin or thicker cuts.

Molleja
Sweetbreads (i.e., the thymus gland of a young lamb or calf). Since antibiotics, hormones, and drugs accumulate in these glands, it's best to avoid these unless you know the meat to be sourced from organic, artisanal, or traditional farms!

Butifarra
A peppery pork sausage. The white variety is made entirely of lean pork, while the black kind is packed with pork fat and blood.

Morcilla (Mex) | Moronga (Carib)
Coagulated blood sausage. Consider yourself warned.

Cuy
Guinea pig. In rural parts of the Andes, you'll find street vendors selling whole roasted guinea pigs out of their carts like hot dogs.

HOW WOULD YOU LIKE YOUR GUINEA PIG COOKED, SIR?
¿CÓMO LE COCINO EL CUY, SEÑOR?

Very rare	*Casi crudo; Sangriento* (bloody)
Rare	*Vuelta y vuelta* (barely flipped twice)
Medium-rare	*Un cuarto*
Medium	*A mitad; A punto*
Medium-well	*Tres cuartos; Más cocido*
Well-done	*Bien cocido*
Burnt to a crisp	*Quemadito; Carbonizado*
Um, I'm a vegetarian.	*Eeeh, soy vegetariano.*

Codorniz

In wooded regions throughout Latin America, don't be surprised to see whole quail on the menu, often fried, roasted, or grilled.

Garrobo

A kind of iguana, usually served in its broth like turtle meat.

Callos

A Spanish form of tripe (i.e., beef stomach) from a younger, less world-weary digestive tract. Mmmm!

Chinchulines

Chunks of barbecued intestine. You may wanna check that they've been completely emptied.

Street food
Comida callejera

Spanish speakers don't go in for fast food the way Americans do. Why deal with fluorescent lights, ugly uniforms, and zit-faced teens when you can buy cheaper food from a grizzled, one-eyed mountain man pushing a griddle around in a shopping cart, or an *abuelita* muttering profanities under her breath like she has late-onset Tourette's? Social dynamics aside, lots of the culinary traditions we associate with Latin America are carb-heavy, portable finger foods, easy to cook in huge quantities and keep warm hygienically for hours, so fast food never really got a foothold because it can't compete financially. Similarly, fast food does almost all its business at lunchtime because bars sell better, cheaper food faster—with alcohol to tip the scales. Ronald McDonald hasn't got a chance.

I'm dying for a good....
Estoy muriendo por un buen....

Taco (Mexico)

Think you know something about tacos just cuz you can pronounce *carne asada*? There are encyclopedic volumes in every Mexican bookstore to show you how much more there is to know. Some of the most common tacos meats are *al pastor* (spicy, spit-roasted pork), *tacos árabes* (in pita bread), tacos stuffed with spicy *papas* (bright-red mashed potatoes), *nopales* (cactus), *buche* (tripe), *ubre* (udder), *cuerno* (horn-skinflap), *bofe* (lung), *suadero* (braised skin-on beef or pork), *trompa* (lips), *cecina* (Southern spicy pork), *tingas* (tomato-stewed), and *sesos* (brains). Makes the menu at your local *taquería* seem a little limited, no?

Huarache (Southern Mexico)

This Aztec forerunner of the modern taco is made thick from fresh yellow or blue corn, shaped like the sole of a sandal (hence the name), stuffed with a layer of black beans, and traditionally topped with cheese, *salsa verde*, sautéed mushrooms, squash flowers, and/or meats.

Pupusa (El Salvador, Honduras, Nicaragua, Guatemala)

This griddle-cake is like a *huarache* but bigger and perfectly round, often filled with *queso y loroco* (the sweet bud of a native vine), *queso y chipilín* (a savory herb), or *revueltas* (a combination of cheese, *chicharrón*, and refried beans). A good *pupusa* will fill you up with breakfasty, comfort-food goodness, while a bad one will have you wincing through greasy burps for a day and a half.

Elote (Central America)

The name *elote* refers specifically to sweet corn. When an *elotero* yells the word on the street, though, they're talkin' 'bout corn on the cob, boiled, roasted, or barbecued on a jerry-rigged shopping cart. Spice it up with 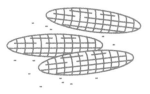 room-temperature mayo, *cotija* cheese, *chilitos*, lime juice, salt, and *Tequesquite* (a pre-Columbian mineral salt).

Tamal (Central America, Andes)

The further south you go, the weirder tamales get. Banana leaf–steamed *tamales yucatecas* are stuffed with pork marrow, annatto seed, and sour orange stew. *Tamales pishques* have refried beans and ash stirred in with the cornmeal masa. The huge, intense Nicaraguan *nacatamal* has annatto-seed pork, rice, potatoes, mint, olives, and raisins. Some Andean tamales include peanuts, turtle meat, and African herbs, while in Northern Argentina, the *masa* is half corn and half squash.

Atol (Central America)

The name *atol* refers to both chowdery soups and hot drinks, often sold out of giant soup thermoses pushed around in a baby stroller. The most common Mexican *atol* is *achampurrado*, a thick, modern form of Aztec hot cocoa (with cinnamon, chile pepper, and whole milk). In many countries you'll get a bowl of savory, bean-watery *atoles* when you buy *pupusas*, whether from a restaurant, a window counter, or some guy with an eye-patch pushing a cart down the street.

Aguafresca (Central America)

These cooling, sugary beverages come in an infinite array of flavors, including hibiscus blossom, mango, watermelon, tamarind, sugarcane, and papaya. You can even still find some of the pre-Columbian *aguasfrescas* like *tepache* (fermented pineapple rind and crude cane), *pinole* (sweet spices and roasted cornmeal), *lechuguilla* (a kind of agave cactus), and *tesgüino* (a malty corn beer). Go for it, young adventurer!

Migas, aka migas de pastor (Southern Spain)

This couscous like dish was traditionally made from hard bread and was cooked in a big pan with bacon or pigskin and a bunch of other meats, veggies, and even sweets like melon, grapes, or chocolate. It's not much to look at when the vendor is stirring it around with a big wooden stick, but trust me, it's legit.

THE NOT-SO-UNIVERSAL LANGUAGE OF GRUB
CON LA COMIDA, HAY POCO UNIVERSAL

GRUB	TO GRUB/CHOW DOWN
El refín (Mex)	*Refinar; Echar papa* (Mex)
El pipirín; El merol (CenAm)	*Jamar* (CenAm)
El papeo; La jala (Spn)	*Jalar; Jamar; Papear* (Spn)
La manya (S.Cone)	*Morfar; Manyar* (S.Cone)
La jama (Andes)	*Jamear; Combear; Papear* (Andes)
La jama; El pasto (Carib)	*Jamar* (Carib)

Ceviche (Perú, Ecuador, Mexico)

Perú is proud of its only major culinary export—few people outside Japan or Polynesia get this excited about raw fish. Ceviche is "cooked" by adding acidic vinegar and lime juice that kill more microbes than most "real" cooking. There are tons of regional variations, like the shellfish- and sea snail–heavy Ecuadorian kind, or the uncannily black *conchas negras* ceviche served in a shell with *plátanos* or *batata* and toasted corn.

Paella (Spain)

This famous rice dish is named after the pan it's cooked in, a huge, shallow vat that evaporates moisture out quickly. The most famous paella, the saffron-laden Valencian kind, takes all day to cook and incorporates as many sea snails and shellfish as the season allows. *Paella mixta* "mixes in" rabbit and chicken with the shellfish. And *arroz negro* is a *paella* dyed black with squid or cuttlefish ink, great for adventurous eaters and cephalopod buffs alike.

Bacalao al pil-pil (Northwestern Spain)

This freaky Basque dish involves slow-cooking big chunks of cod, garlic, and tiny chile peppers in tons of olive oil until the oil congeals into a gelatinous sauce. Basque doesn't have a word for the texture, which is probably why they made up the onomatopoetic *pil-pil*. Or maybe someone just tried to trick their kids into eating it by giving it a cutesy name, because honestly, it's pretty gross.

Plátanos, aka tajadas (Caribbean, Central America)

Fried plantains get cut in strips (*tajadas*) to maximize the frying area *and* your cholesterol. Beware of *patacón pisao*, though: the deep-fried green plantain peel can be too weird for people that didn't grow up eating plaintains. *Tostones*, on the other hand, are delicious since they're mashed halfway through cooking to get a nice, varied texture.

Biónico

A fancy and "energizing" Mexican fruit salad with cream, granola, and sometimes fancy toppings like shredded coconut and nuts or seeds, sometimes eaten as a dessert, meal alternative, or just as a healthier second course when that first course of street-food hits your stomach punishingly.

Other grub
Otras manducas

Let's face it, Spanish speakers are Catholics, and Catholics have a lot of mouths to feed. And there's no more efficient way to use all the scraps in the fridge than to throw together a sandwich, make a stew, or stuff last night's leftovers into some dough and bake it in the oven.

I don't need a complete meal, I'm fine with **small plates** at the pub.
*No necesito una comida entera, me alcanzan unas **tapas** en el bar.*

Go make me a...sandwich.
Anda a hacerme un sandwich....

Cubano (Caribbean)
The porkiest sandwich on earth! To make an old-school *cubano*, you take a roll shortened with pig-lard, warm it in pig-lard on a griddle, and add Swiss cheese, ham, and roast pork.

De miga (Argentina, Uruguay)
A crustless sandwich made from paper-thin slices of white bread, heavy on the mayo. The traditional fillings are ham, processed cheese, slices of oily pepper and/or palm hearts, lettuce, tomato, and an olivey egg salad. Throw one into a panini grill and you have the best snack ever invented, known simply as *un tostado*.

Pintxos (Basque Spain, Galicia)

This term refers to all kinds of open-faced mini-sandwiches, mostly on slices of baguette, but sometimes breadless or on pastry, as is traditional to Western Spain's bars, as opposed to the less bread-centric *tapas* of the rest of Spain. They come out of the kitchen on huge trays that bar-goers snatch up like boat-sushi, with similar systems of plate-counting when time comes to pay your bill. Not for the shellfish-averse—the most traditional proteins for *pintxos* are salt cod, octopus, and sea snails.

De jamón serrano, aka jamón curado (Spain)

The ham in these sandwiches is dried and salt-cured for one to two years in whole hocks that often hang over the counter in a bar or deli. The prized *ibérico* variety is cured longer and made from pigs raised on a diet of grass and acorns (*bellotas*). Pair this with some dry cheese and you're in for a world-class sandwich—but remember to check the price before ordering, because the fancier varieties cost a lot more than you might be used to paying for cold deli meats.

Pambazo (Guadalajara)

This gut-busting local variation on the Mexican *torta* (a lighter "Cuban" with avocado, raw onion, and beans) ups the heartburn ante with peppery *chorizo*, mashed potatoes, and a hyperbolically messy hot-sauce bath.

Let's stew up some....
Pongámonos a guisar un/una....

Locro (Argentina, Bolivia, Paraguay)

A thick-as-peanut-butter stew featuring hominy, beans, and often-tendony shredded meat scraps. When done right, it's like an amazing French *cassoulet*—but when it's done wrong, it feels like you're eating mess hall slop in a WWI movie.

Ropa vieja (Cuba)

Fancy shredded pork stewed in a tomato-based *criollo* sauce, with the texture of the tattered rags you can't even use for cleaning anymore, hence the name "old clothes."

Menudo (Mexico)

Most of the organs in this stew (including the free-floating eyeballs in some recipes) retain their shape and gaze up at you, whole, from your bowl. Consider yourself warned.

Mondongo (Local variations in every country in Latin America)

A tripe-forward stew made with exotic tubers (yucca, cornmeal cakes, purple potatoes) and veggies. Few of the many variations will appeal to you, however, if you're not a fan of tripe and haggis.

Posole aka pozol (Southern Mexico, Honduras, Guatemala)

A pork stew with hominy and pig organs slow-cooked in a chile-chicken broth. At the last minute, you dump in tons of fresh oregano, lime juice, and onion. Traditional at weddings and banquets, the guest of honor gets a big piece of pig's face in their bowl, and as everyone lines up at the ladle for their bowl, the four guests who get a pig's foot are blessed with years of good luck (or something).

Mote (Andes)

Although the term can refer to any number of grains cooked any number of ways, the most common *mote* refers either to the boiled hominy served with Peruvian ceviche or to the thick, heavily seasoned hominy soups made from the same varieties and often sold as a street food in Andean Ecuador, Colombia, and Perú.

Chupe (Bolivia, Perú, Colombia, Paraguay, Chile, Panamá)

This is a general term for various buttery, white soups made with barley, corn, or other grains, plus enough big chunks of meat that you'll need a knife to go along with your spork.

Olla podrida (Western Spain)

The name of the dish literally means, "putrid pot," although some people speculate it's a corruption of *poderida* ("fortified"). It's a rich red-bean stew, "fortified" and thickened by bacon, blood sausage, smoked pig's ear, ribs, and snout. Nothing says delicious like snout.

YOU SAY TOMATO, I SAY JÍTOMATE

Throughout Latin America, particularly where each indigenous language is native, many fruits and veggies are still called by their pre-Columbian names instead of their standard Spanish ones.

Tomato (the big, firm kind)	*Jítomate (Nahuatl)*
Peanut	*Maní (Taino)*
Chili pepper	*Ají (Taino)*
Squash	*Ayote (Nahuatl), Pipián (Mayan), Zapallo (Quechua)*
Sweet potato	*Camote (Nahuatl), Boniato (Taino)*
Corn	*Elote (Nahuatl), Choclo (Quechua)*
Avocado	*Aguacate (Nahuatl), Palta (Quechua)*

Your mom sure knows how to bake a mean....
Sí que tu vieja sabe hornear un/a buen/a....

Sope, aka pellizcada, picadita (Mexico)

This is like a taco-pizza—almost twice as large as a taco, thicker (and still soft and gooey inside), turned up at the edges like a pizza crust, and topped evenly instead of mounded like a taco.

Gordita (Mexico)

Imagine a hot-pocket made by flash-frying a stuffed hand-made tortilla, then cutting it in half and stuffing in cheese while it's still hot enough to melt it, then baking it to a crisp.

Empanada (Southern Cone, Colombia)

The Argentine variety are like a hand-held calzone. They're usually filled with ham and cheese, spiced meat, spinach, or *humita* (a sweet corn white sauce). Chilean ones are more like flaky meat turnovers, and Colombian ones are like English potpies, usually fried instead of baked. Central Americans use the term for any number of baked things, from oven-quesadillas to pies to casseroles.

I've got a bit of a sweet tooth. I could really go for some/a....
Soy medio goloso. Estoy antojando....

Helado de mamey

When you're in tropical regions, a healthy distrust of local dairy products is both logical and recommended: As a seasoned backpacker once told me, "Don't eat ice cream anywhere refrigeration costs more than health care." One exception I recommend making to this axiom is for ice cream made with the Caribbean's weirdest, pulpiest fruit, the *mamey*, which is like a ripe papaya that tastes like strawberries but hides inside a coconut shell. Other exotic fruit flavors of ice cream worth try trying include: South American *guanabana* (aka "soursop"), the smaller Mexican *chirimoya*, Peruvian *lúcuma* (even pastier!), and local varieties of *higo* (fig).

Horchata

The only ingredients that the various Spanish, Mexican, and Andean varieties of this sweet dessert and/or beverage share are water and rice flour of some kind. Beyond that, you really don't know what you're ordering until you drink it. Walnuts (Oaxaca) and almonds (Andalucía) might be floating in it; it might be disgustingly sweet or refreshingly watery or kind of savory; it might have cinnamon, cloves, nutmeg, allspice, or even artificial cinnamon syrup (i.e., liquid Red Hots); it might be piping hot, lukewarm, or full of ice. Just think of it as weird, wholesome rice milk.

Crema catalana

Don't let a proud Cataluñian hear you call it crème brûlée—they're pretty confident that they invented it and that the French ripped them off. The Cataluñian original doesn't have the carbonized sugar crust, for better or for worse, although some form of liquid caramel is usually present in its place.

Manjar blanco

This debatably pre-Colombian Peruvian treat is a dense, layered combination of toffee, milk caramel, and shortbread. There are regional variations all over the country (many using exotic caramels made from the milk of goats, sheep, or even llamas), but any way you slice it, your dentist doesn't want you eating it—it's pretty much guaranteed to end up deeply entrenched in your grill.

Alfajores

Across the Spanish-speaking world, there are boatloads of dry, crumbly cookies and biscuits that share this (notably Arabic) name. In Argentina in particular, however, it has been elevated it to the level of a national art form. The classical Argentine version consists of a huge gob of *dulce de leche* (rich milk caramel) or, in some cases, regional fruit jam between two cookies or scone like biscuits. Since the nineteenth century, chocolate-coated, coconut-dusted, and/or meringue-covered variations have been competing in a Cold War of regional specialties and niche markets; a group of alfanerds in Buenos Aires even run a blog rating the hundreds of licensed manufacturers nationwide, proving the old adage: Nothing really exists until a group of nerds obsess over it on the Internet.

Churros

Even though the longer, cinnamon-heavy variety has been a staple of Mexican county fairs and Mexican-

American restaurants for generations, Mexican foodies will usually begrudgingly acknowledge that the *original* churros are short, unspiced *churros madrileños* dating back to before the conquest. What's harder is getting a nationalistic Spaniard to acknowledge the resemblance between churros and similar-looking North African fried desserts. (What's even more curious is that the oldest and most famous churro restaurant in Mexico's capital is called El Moro and decorated beautifully in traditional Andalucian, i.e., Arabic, tiles. Go figure!) In all three cultural contexts, the natural habitat of the churro is a chilly night and near a cup of hot cocoa—perfect for staying cozy between meals, or, if you're in a different stage of your life, for soaking up that ninth whiskey while you wait for the trains to start running again.

Agarapiñadas (Spn, S.Cone) | *Garapiñado* (Mex)

When you think "Spanish peanuts," you probably think of those disgusting packaged sugar-coated peanuts you get at truck stops when you're too drunk or stoned to reason clearly about your snacking options. Those pathetic American nut bags are, in fact, descended from a noble line of caramelized nuts (usually peanuts, but sometimes almonds, walnuts, hazelnuts, or a combination), which are traditionally sold from steaming street carts or, in rare cases, packaged and served cold. The secret ingredient is baking soda, which makes the caramel bubble and blister as it heats—only to cool rapidly into that satisfyingly brittle texture.

[Pastel de] Tres Leches

No one knows exactly where the *tres leches* comes from, but in all its variations, this cream-based pastry has a distinctly airy texture and about as much saturated fat per serving as is humanly possible without butter or lard. It's kind of like a 1950s tiramisu, except sweeter and often alcoholic. The name refers to the three forms of "milk" that you combine with flour before baking: canned evaporated milk, canned condensed milk, and either heavy whipping cream (Mex, Spn) or coconut "cream" (Carib). As if that weren't intense enough, many pastry chefs keep going by piling on additional "creams": whipped cream topping, molasses, rum, and brandy being the most common. (These last two often change the name to *pastel borracho* for obvious reasons.)

Mazamorra

Technically, this term refers to an Incan method for milling cornmeal that survives in many forms, but it most often designates a corn pudding ubiquitous in Perú. It's sweetened with cane sugar and dyed naturally by a kind of high-elevation purple corn that produces even stronger purple hues than beets do. Some of the more savory variations got Paraguay through the six-year food shortage of the Three Alliances war, while an *horchata*-like beverage by the same name accompanies the typical dish of the Colombian highlanders, the *bandeja paisa*. Basically, the term means "homemade corn syrup that dyes your teeth purple."

Acknowledgments

I wish I had the space and recollection to thank everyone who helped me with this book, but circumstances conspire against it. Chapters and entire draft copies were reviewed by Caballeros María and Carlos, Victor Goldgel Carballo, Gabrielle Wolodarski, Ignacio Gatto Bellora, and Jorge Díaz-Velez. Roxana Fitch's website and the forum posters on wordreference.com also made this book possible, as did any number of anonymous wiki-ers, *piroperos*, smart-asses, graffiti artists, poets, and criminals. The third edition was helped substantially by my assistant editor Elana Banafshe-Johnson and the students of my translation workshop at Earlham College. And thanks to Professor (now emeritus) Francine Masiello and her habitual overconfidence in my abilities for initially recommending me to the fine people at Ulysses.

About the Author

Juan Caballero is an assistant professor in the Department of Spanish and Hispanic Studies at Earlham College in Richmond, Indiana. His academic research has spanned the Argentine novel, psychoanalysis, sadomasochism, linguistics, film noir, Third-World aesthetics, and socialist revisionism. He is a lifelong Californian and avid backpacker, whose passions include competitive eating, contemporary art, noise music, booty-shakin', and road-tripping.

9 781646 043958